# INFLATION

## A STUDY IN
## ECONOMICS, ETHICS, AND POLITICS

THE COLVER LECTURES
IN BROWN UNIVERSITY
1957

# INFLATION

## A STUDY IN
## *Economics, Ethics, and Politics*

### G. L. BACH

PROVIDENCE · RHODE ISLAND

Brown University Press
1958

*Library of Congress Catalog Card Number: 57-14977*

COMPOSED, PRINTED AND BOUND BY
GEORGE BANTA CO., INC., MENASHA, WISCONSIN

# PREFACE

THE SUBSTANCE of this little book was delivered as the Colver Lectures in Brown University in February of 1957, and I have left the language largely in the informal style of the lectures. The book is intended, as were the lectures, primarily for the layman who is interested in one of the major economic, ethical, and political problems of our day—inflation. It provides a summary of the major facts and issues involved in the problem and, I hope, some suggestions for public policy that may be stimulating and provocative for the serious citizen. I have left unchanged the language and introductory sections so that the chapters can be read separately as well as consecutively, as was my object with the lectures.

There is little economics in the book that will be novel to the professional economist. For him its usefulness is more likely to be as a brief organized statement of the major issues and some of the central facts in the inflation problem. But I venture to hope that some of the analysis relating the economic aspects of inflation to our modern social and political processes may be interesting to him too. My purpose extends beyond economics.

In a volume of this sort, one's indebtedness is inevitably far-reaching and hard to identify. I have been interested in this problem for many years, and this little volume has presented an opportunity to summarize in non-technical form some of the suggestions I have made earlier and the conclusions to which I have been drawn, as well as to pull together the ideas of other writers. The obvious parallelism between some of my analysis and that of Professor Martin Bronfenbrenner is noted in the text, as is the similarity in one major area to an analysis of the *London Economist* some years ago. Part of the material in Chapter 1 is based on a more elaborate analysis of the economic effects of inflation that I published recently (with Albert Ando) in the *Review of Economics and Statistics*.

It is a pleasure to acknowledge the generosity of the Colver Lecture Fund of Brown University in arranging the publication of these lectures, in this slightly expanded form; and the generous assistance of Professor George Borts of Brown in reviewing the manuscript for publication. I am indebted to David Chambers for the index.

G. L. B.

Pittsburgh, Pennsylvania
May, 1957

# Table of Contents

# I  The Economic Impact
## of Inflation

WE LIVE, IT IS SAID, in an age of inflation. Over the past two decades, prices in the United States have roughly doubled. That is, the buying power of one dollar over a market basket of typical cost-of-living items is only half of what it was in 1937. In no major nation of the world have prices risen by less than about this amount. In many, prices have risen far more. In the United Kingdom, for example, the cost of living has risen about 150 percent over the period. One British pound will buy about 40 percent of what it would command in 1937. In Brazil, the cost of living is now approximately fifteen times as high as in 1937. One cruzeiro will buy only about 7 percent as much as twenty years ago.

Much of this world-wide inflation occurred during World War II. But much of it has occurred since the war's end. In this country prices have risen by about 40 percent since mid-1946. Among the nations on which we have reasonably reliable information, only a few of the smaller countries have shown appreciably smaller post-war price rises. Table 1 shows the post-war decline in the buying power of the monetary unit in a world-wide sample of countries. In each case, the average annual rate of depreciation in the value of money over the decade is also shown. For example, one Swedish kroner would buy about two-thirds as much in 1956 as a decade earlier, a decline of about 4.2 percent per year in its buying power over a decade.

TABLE 1
THE FALLING VALUE OF MONEY, 1946–56[a]

| Country | Value of Money[b] | | Annual Rate of Depreciation[c] |
|---|---|---|---|
| | 1946 | 1956 | |
| Switzerland | 100 | 86 | 1.5% |
| Germany | 100 | 72 | 3.2 |
| India | 100 | 72 | 3.2 |
| United States | 100 | 71 | 3.4 |
| Venezuela | 100 | 70 | 3.5 |
| Netherlands | 100 | 67 | 4.0 |
| Canada | 100 | 65 | 4.2 |
| Sweden | 100 | 65 | 4.2 |
| United Kingdom | 100 | 65 | 4.2 |
| France | 100 | 58 | 6.5 |
| Mexico | 100 | 47 | 7.4 |
| Australia | 100 | 46 | 7.5 |
| Brazil | 100 | 26 | 12.7 |
| Chile | 100 | 5 | 25.3 |

[a] Data are official cost-of-living figures in most cases.
[b] For each country the 1956 figure is the value of the country's monetary unit compared to its 1946 buying power.
[c] Annual rate is compounded.

Indeed, if we look at the broad sweep of world history, the amazing thing is that man has not long since come to expect inflation as the normal event, and a continuing stable value of his monetary unit the exception. Inflation has vexed nations and their rulers since the earliest days of recorded history. And no nation of the modern world has avoided a major drop in the real purchasing power of its monetary unit. In many cases, the drop has practically wiped out the buying power of the nation's monetary unit.

Not that prices have risen steadily. They have not. There have been long valleys between the steep peaks of inflation in many nations, and there is a striking coincidence between major wars and major inflations. But in every country, the net result over the decades has been a persistent uptrend of prices.)

## I

Most major American groups appear to be against inflation. President Eisenhower and ex-President Truman; the CIO-AFL and the National Association of Manufacturers; the Committee for Economic Development and the Farm Bureau —all have stressed the importance of preserving the purchasing power of the American dollar. Yet the reasons why these diverse groups oppose inflation are many, and often muddled, if we are to judge from the statements of their leaders.

Inflation bleeds the little fellow and the working man. It increases profits at the expense of wages—or it transfers profits to the wage earner. It lowers the national standard of living. It leads inevitably to boom, bust and depression. It transfers income and wealth from the poor to the rich—or from the rich to the poor. It wipes out the value of savings and induces waste and dissolution. These are only a few of the claims gleaned from a casual reading of the daily papers and a sampling of the history books and campaign speeches of recent years. Nor is there any clear consensus among professional economists as to just who gains and who loses how much from inflation.

Indeed, over the past few years the voice of the infidel has been heard in the temple of sound money. Maybe a little inflation now and then is a good thing—to stimulate economic progress and to prod the rentier class to do some work, rather than living comfortably off the rest of us through no greater exertion than clipping bond coupons. And this suggestion comes not as a coarse whisper from some unwashed radical, nor as a strident shout from ardent inflationists like the Green-backers and the Populists of the 19th century. Indeed, it has come from the very pinnacle of respectability—Professor Sumner Slichter, perhaps the best known member of the Harvard Business School and Economics Department faculties and the most influential "business man's economist" of our day.

Nor is Professor Slichter the only doubter. Several other influential economists, primarily of Keynesian and "guaranteed full employment" persuasion, have hinted at the Slichter position—though they seldom espouse inflation outright. Professor Earl Hamliton of the University of Chicago has argued learnedly in a series of important historical articles that the standard of living of the western world has risen fastest when gentle inflation has prevailed. And scratch many a business-man, farmer, or working man, and you will find not far under his surface pronouncements against inflation a willingness to have a quick sip of the forbidden drink—so long as he doesn't have to admit it publicly.[1]

It will be one of my main theses that inflation is likely to

[1] Many words have been written about the economic effects of inflation. Some of the leading studies are the following: On the post-war hyper-inflations of central Europe: C. Bresciani-Turroni, *The Economics of Inflation* (G. Allen and Unwin, 1937), and Frank Graham, *Exchange, Prices, and Production in Hyper-Inflation: Germany, 1920-1923* (Princeton University Press, 1930). On the long sweep of inflation over the centuries: Earl Hamilton, "Prices As a Factor in Business Growth," *Journal of Economic History*, Fall, 1952; and David Felix, "Profit Inflation and Industrial Growth," *Quarterly Journal of Economics*, August, 1956. On recent effects in America and abroad: Sumner Slichter, "How Bad Is Inflation?" *Harpers Magazine*, August, 1952; G. L. Bach and Albert Ando, "The Redistributional Effects of Inflation," *Review of Economics and Statistics*, February, 1957; R. C. Jones, *Effects of Price Level Changes on Business Income, Capital, and Taxes* (American Accounting Association, 1956); and J. M. Grant and R. L. Mathews, "The Effects of Inflation on Company Profits and Financial Structures," *Economic Record*, May, 1956. Several other theoretical and empirical studies are referred to later on.

be a major social phenomenon of the half century ahead. If this is correct, it is important to analyze carefully and objectively just what the economic effects of inflation have been in the past. This may help to settle some of the conflicting claims about this controversial subject, and it may help provide a basis for reasoned judgments about alternative steps to prevent—or conceivably encourage—inflation in the future.

This is the basic task I have set myself in this opening chapter—to look at the economic impact of inflation on the American economy, primarily over the past two decades, but also more hurriedly during earlier times in America, and at experiences abroad. I am afraid that this kind of objective examination of facts, inescapably complex on some points, may be somewhat lacking in glamour—though some of the conclusions may be surprising. But I know of no way to examine responsibly the trends leading into the future or the alternative courses of public policy toward inflation without beginning with a hard look at the facts.

In the following chapter, then, I propose to peer into the future, looking at what seems to me to be the major likely trend of inflation over the decades ahead.

In the final chapters, I shall be concerned primarily with the fascinating intermesh of economics, ethics, and politics which an age of inflation inescapably encounters in a democratic society like ours. For I shall argue that inflation, if it continues in the future, as I suspect it will, will be by no means exclusively an economic phenomenon. Rather, its roots will lie deep within our political and social processes and values. And public policy toward inflationary pressures, I shall argue, must be developed and assessed in this frame of reference, rather than merely as a problem in applied economics.

## II

One reason why arguments about inflation so often get no-where except around a circle is that the disputants so often fail to define the term. It is hardly a novel pronouncement that careful definition of terms is an essential first step in any orderly discussion of complex phenomena. Yet to emphasize the obvious may be forgivable here. A compendium of definitions from leading dictionaries, encyclopedias and textbooks makes the area look like a veritable no man's land. Hardly any two are alike in all important respects, and the variation is enormous, even to the point of some authors' pointing out specifically how foolish the definitions of others are.

I trust I need not labor the pointlessness of argument over which definition is "right." My test of a good definition is whether it is useful in forwarding our analysis and in permitting us to communicate effectively about the problem. Thus, I do not argue that the definition I propose is necessarily the best of all definitions (though it seems so to me); but merely that it is a useful definition which can help us analyze the problems at hand, and that it is simple and clear, a virtue of no small importance in this confused field of allegation, fact and fiction.

By inflation, I shall mean a rise in the price level, or (what is the same thing) a fall in the purchasing power of the monetary unit. Economists will recognize immediately the problem of deciding *what* price level and how to measure it. I do not wish to minimize the importance of this problem for many purposes, but I think it will become clear that for most of what I have to say it is not crucial, so long as we choose a broad-based price index that is widely representative of commodity and service prices at the wholesale or retail level (excluding wage rates, the price of labor). I shall generally use the well-known Bureau of Labor Statistics index of consumer prices to measure price level changes, recognizing that this measures directly only prices of goods and services entering the "cost of living" of lower middle income families in selected cities. The broader Bureau of Labor Statistics wholesale price index can be substituted without changing significantly the conclusions reported.

Two special notes of warning are needed on this definition, to prevent misunderstanding. First, the definition says that inflation *is* a rise in prices—not that rising prices are merely a *symptom* of inflation. Those who reject the simple definition I propose generally argue that it is, in some sense, an overextension of money and credit that "causes" rising prices, and that it is this overissue of money that *is* the inflation. This is, of course, a permissible definition of inflation. Under it, inflation may or may not be associated with a rising price level, and rising prices may or may not be associated with inflation. But permissible though that definition may be, I shall not use it, partly because it does not seem to me operationally clear (what is "overissue" of money?), and partly because I suspect that it is the rising prices, *per se,* that most people think of when they hear "inflation." This does not, of course, deny that the supply of money and credit relative to the goods and services available for purchase may be a powerful force pushing the price level up or down.

Second, under my definition inflation can occur either with or without full employment. Ordinarily the price level does not rise very rapidly unless reasonably full employment of men and machines prevails. But inflation with partial unemployment is indeed possible under this definition, and it may be increasingly likely over the years ahead, if certain elements of my analysis are correct. Moreover, under this definition, of course, prices need not rise rapidly or explosively for there to be inflation. A small price rise is a little inflation; a larger price rise is a larger inflation.[2]

## III

So much for the problem of definition. Now, what are the economic effects of inflation?

It is convenient to examine the economic effects of inflation, like other economy-wide phenomena, by asking two major questions. First, what effect does inflation have on the *total volume* of goods and services being produced—on the "real gross national product" or the "real national income"? Second, what effect does it have on the *distribution* of those goods and services among the various individuals and groups in society? For example, does it increase the relative share of wages and decrease that of profits? Does it increase the relative share of the well-to-do and decrease that of the poor? Does it increase the relative share of the active workers and decrease that of the "nonworkers," such as retired couples living on pensions? And so on for the shares of any groups in which we may be especially interested.[3]

[2] Some economists prefer a definition that specifies the cause of the price rise and limits inflation to cases after substantially full employment has been reached. For example: Inflation is a rising price level due to expanding monetary demand when unemployment is less than 4-5 percent of the labor force. While this definition has some advantages, it is often non-operational because it is often impossible to define with certainty whether "expanding monetary demand" is the "cause" of the rising prices. Moreover, the effects of rising prices in periods of less than full employment are also important and need analysis just as do rising prices in periods of full employment. For those who wish to distinguish, the cases of inflation with unemployment and with full employment can readily be handled separately, using the simple, more general definition of inflation used in the text.

[3] It is also important to consider the allocation of productive re-

In assessing the evidence on these questions we are immediately up against the age-old problems of generalization and prediction in the social sciences.

(1) Obviously, we cannot look at all past inflations in order to arrive at generalizations as to the effect of inflation. A modest sample must do.

(2) Even if we could look at all cases, we would find that the effect seems to be different at different times. This leaves us, at best, with a *conditional* set of generalizations—if A, then certain results; if B, then other results; and so on.

(3) Since we cannot isolate inflation and its effects in a laboratory, we can never be *sure* whether the results we observe in any given period are *caused* by inflation during the same or a preceding period, or by some other set of circumstances. The fact that higher national output follows inflation, for example, may or may not mean that it was caused by the inflation, even if the sequence appears a number of times.

(4) In the last analysis, we are really interested in the future, not the past. Even if we are reasonably sure about the effects of inflation in the past, can we be reasonably sure that the same effects will recur in the future? This problem, of course, is a complex one, that most social scientists would try to handle with a combination of careful observation of a generous sample of past be-

---

sources between "consumers'" and "producers'" goods. That is, to what extent does inflation lead to more production of goods for current consumption, as against production of factories, machinery, and so on, which will increase the output of consumers' goods only in the future? This question is important for both the level and the distribution of current output.

havior, plus a theory explaining this past behavior in a way that systematically relates inflation to the observed results. Hopefully, the result will be a reasonably reliable conditional prediction: *If* a certain amount of inflation occurs under condition A in the future, *then* the effect on national income will probably be this; *if* the same amount of inflation occurs under condition B, *then* the effect will probably be that; and so on.

In a brief, non-technical treatment, it is obvious that some drastic oversimplification is in order. I propose to state first four very simple, but important, possible relationships between inflation and total national output, and then to summarize very briefly some evidence bearing on these relationships, or hypotheses. I shall follow the same general procedure on the redistributional effects of inflation later on. I must beg the indulgence here of those who want a more rigorous and elaborate statement of hypotheses and their tests.

## IV

Consider first, then, the effect of inflation on the economy's total output, which I shall briefly though not quite accurately call the "national real income." Imagine the national real income as a huge pie of real goods and services. We want to consider whether inflation either increases or decreases significantly the total size of the pie, without concern at the moment for who gets what size slice. Remember that the pie is real goods and services. The money value of any year's pie can be raised merely by bidding up prices, but this would merely raise the national money income, not the nation's *real* income.

Four main lines of argument as to how inflation may affect the size of total national real income have been emphasized:

(1) Inflation may *decrease* the size of the *current* national income, through disrupting normal economic relationships and diverting people from productive activity.

(2) Inflation may *decrease future* national income because inflation may necessarily be followed by deflation and depression, which means mass unemployment of men and machines.

(3) Inflation may *increase current* national real income, through (a) increasing profit margins as wages and other costs lag behind rising prices, thereby stimulating employment and output, (b) inducing people to work longer and harder in order to protect the real purchasing power of their incomes against diminution as inflation erodes the purchasing power of any given number of dollars, and (c) stimulating buying ahead because further price increases are expected. (By "current," I mean here, now or in the immediate future—say, within a year.)

(4) Inflation may *increase* national real income over the *long future* by stimulating the rate of saving and capital accumulation; or it may *decrease* real income over the *long future* by discouraging saving and capital accumulation. That is, it may affect the rate of long-run economic growth.

(1) Consider the first argument, that inflation reduces the size of the *current* national income.

This finds little support in careful *a priori* reasoning; and the evidence of history is flatly against it, *except* in cases of extremely violent runaway, or hyper-, inflation. The popular picture of inflation often traces back to the massive hyper-inflations of central Europe following World War I, when currency became substantially worthless, a basketful of money was needed to buy a loaf of bread, and spending money immediately on receipt became as important as earning it. Under these extreme circumstances, people spent more and more of their time spending money as fast as possible, before its value vanished as prices soared. Production became less important than spending. Speculative activity became more rewarding than work of the usual productive sorts. By 1923 in Germany, for example, this diversion of energy from normal productive work had become a vast drag on the production of real goods and services.

But even in such violent inflations, another fact is striking. It was only in late 1923, after years of drastic inflation that reached astronomical proportions by 1922, that the total size of the German national real output actually fell. This decline preceded the complete collapse of the Germany economy and its financial structure by only a few months. The evidence for other great hyper-inflations, where we have data of any reliability, seems to show a similar pattern—that rapid inflation indeed disrupts normal economic activity and diverts energies from more productive work to seeking protection against inflation, but that even this disruption does not over-balance the incentives to work and produce until the economy approaches a stage approaching complete collapse.

The evidence on milder inflations is reasonably clear: history shows output generally *rising* in periods of inflation. In the United States since 1937, for example, prices have roughly doubled, but the money value of our national income has risen to about 400 percent of 1937. That is, total real output has more than doubled. This pattern of increased real output with rising prices has prevailed in America in each of the three major inflationary bursts within the last two decades. And a similar picture has prevailed in most other periods of American history, and in relatively mild inflations in other countries

—for example, in almost all of non-communist Europe over the same period.

In periods beginning with substantial unemployment, real output has often increased rapidly as prices have risen. Once substantially full employment has been reached, real output has grown more slowly, as the total productive capacity of the economy has increased only gradually. But cases of moderate inflation accompanied by an appreciable drop in total real output have been rare indeed.

These facts, of course, do not prove that the inflation was not exerting a downward pressure on output that was persistently overcome by other expansive forces in these instances. But they do indicate that if this was the situation, the output-depressive impact of inflation has generally been a relatively weak one.

((2) The argument that inflation reduces *future* real output by creating a boom and bust situation runs roughly as follows, though I am drastically oversimplifying the more sophisticated versions of the argument. Rising prices lead to expectations of further increases. This leads to forward buying and speculative activity, especially to the accumulation of business and consumer inventories beyond actual immediate needs. But such a speculative boom can be supported only temporarily, since speculative purchases are in excess of expected needs or are for resale on the assumption that someone else will require them and be willing to pay a still higher price. Overbuying on the basis of expected future inflation must ultimately collapse; paper profits cannot provide a permanently rising price structure. And the collapse, when it comes, will, as a practical matter, often bring general collapse in business spending, unemployment, and depression.)

What is the evidence? It provides both support for the argument and contradiction to it. To say that inflation *must* be followed directly by collapse and depression is clearly wrong. For example, in Brazil, which has had substantially continuous inflation over the past two decades averaging over 10 percent per annum, total real output in the economy has grown persistently. In France, where prices have nearly doubled over the past ten years real output has grown steadily. In the United Kingdom, with a 50 percent increase in prices, the picture is the same. Here in the United States, substantial inflation since World War II, concentrated largely in 1946-48 and 1950-51, has been paralleled by a huge growth in real national income. It is clear that inflation does not necessarily presage collapse and unemployment just around the corner—certainly not around a very nearby corner.

On the other hand, sharp inflations have sometimes been followed by price collapses apparently arising from the excesses of speculative price increases, often fed by large-scale bank borrowing. The sharp 1920-21 collapse in the United States following the big World War I inflation is a good case in point. Such cases, interestingly, are easier to find during the 19th and early 20th centuries than during the past quarter century.

Conclusion: A Scotch verdict. (Rapid inflation *may* lead to a price collapse and ensuing unemployment. But history provides a large number of counter-examples, where persistent inflation at different rates has been accompanied over long periods by rising total real output.)

(3) How about the third argument—that inflation *increases* current real national income? This generally rests on three points. (a) Inflation may increase profits as selling prices rise faster than costs (especially than wages), and the increase in profits may stimulate business investment spending and em-

*14*

ployment. (b) Inflation gradually erodes the real purchasing power of relatively fixed incomes, such as pensions and interest on bonds. This pressure may force "non-workers" who live on such fixed incomes to return to productive employment. More important, it may force others whose money incomes lag to work harder or longer. For example, laborers may take part-time second jobs, wives may enter the labor force to supplement the family income, and workers in jobs where consumer demand has languished may move to better paying employers. (c) *Expectation* of continued inflation may stimulate buying now to anticipate the expected higher prices. This may mean more spending by both businesses and individuals than would occur without inflation, and may thus increase employment and production. This point, of course, rests on *expectation* of *continued* inflation, not on inflation itself. It is important to note that the first and third of these points are valid only if unemployment of men or machines exists in the economy; otherwise the increased spending will merely bid up prices further. The second point may be valid under either full or underemployment conditions.

What does the evidence show? Evaluation here is difficult. There is no doubt that output has generally risen in inflation periods. But the conclusion does not necessarily follow that inflation has generally, or ever, *caused* the rising output. Output has also risen in periods of stable, or even slightly declining, prices; the 1920's in the United States are a leading example. Indeed, with a growing labor force, capital accumulation, and improving technology, total national output must be expected to rise persistently over the years, and at a substantial rate of perhaps 2 to 4 percent annually in the United States. Unless it does increase at something like this rate, we can anticipate steadily mounting depression and unemployment, as new workers entering the labor force fail to find jobs and old workers are laid off through technological advance which permits the same output to be turned up by ever fewer workers. Thus, to see inflation and increased output together by no means automatically throws the credit to rising prices. Consider the sub-arguments separately.

( (a) The major support for the "inflation increases output" argument in periods of unemployment lies in the wage-lag hypothesis. Inflation, it is argued, stimulates production, investment, and employment through increasing profits, as wages (and other costs) lag behind rising prices.) But, as I shall argue below, this hypothesis is not supported by modern evidence. Wages have lagged substantially behind rising product prices in many past inflations. But not in the United States of today, except possibly very temporarily in a sharp spurt of prices as at the outbreak of the Korean War.

And this situation is by no means limited to the United States. Wages throughout the western industrialized world seem to be increasingly mobile upward, in many instances linked to rising prices through built-in "escalator" clauses. Thus the major analytical support for the inflation stimulus to increased output finds shaky support in the evidence of the modern world. Clearly, the wage-lag is more likely in a depressed, unemployment economy than in a fully employed one —and perhaps the wage-lag has vanished only temporarily in the full employment world of the past decade. But I suspect that the substantially full-employment world itself is not so temporary.

Some other costs may lag in inflation, even though wages do not. Interest charges, rents, salaries, and other costs are temporarily fixed in dollar terms as selling prices of business products rise. But there is little evidence that these lags are as long as they once were; and they can easily be overcome by only a modest wage-lead, since wages, directly or indirectly, generally comprise the largest component of total cost.

(Perhaps more important, inflation leads to substantial overstatement of profits under prevailing accounting practices. Depreciation charges on plant and equipment are generally computed on original cost. When prices rise depreciation funds are inadequate to replace the wearing out equipment.) Part of what appears to be profit is, in effect, uncharged depreciation since the money must be used to supplement depreciation reserves in buying new plant and equipment. Similarly, when materials inventory used in production must be replaced at higher prices, "real" profits will be overstated unless the replacement cost rather than the original cost is used in computing profits. Estimates presented in more detail below suggest that "real" corporate profits may have been overstated by as much as one-third during the post-war inflation because of these factors. While businessmen complain vigorously that they are overtaxed because they must pay on these phantom profits as well as on "real" profits, nevertheless the existence of large accounting money profits may stimulate them to increased investment spending beyond that which would be induced by the "real" profit figures. On this point, see (4) below.

(b) How about the argument that inflation drives lagging income groups, especially non-workers, to work more and harder in order to protect their real income? Casual observation turns up a variety of cases where this is true—retired men who have been driven back to part-time work, wives of college professors working to supplement their husbands' lagging salaries, school teachers driving taxis or working in industry during summer "vacations." But it is less clear that the effect is a far-reaching one, at least for moderate inflation.

The effect of inflation in inducing more work from lagging income groups depends on several interrelated factors. One is how fast the value of money is eroding. Another is how far behind prices incomes lag; if the lag is great, the pressure to step up income-earning activities is correspondingly greater. Another is how important the lagging income groups are in the economy—if no major income groups lag substantially, clearly no large amount of additional labor can be produced by inflation via this channel. The last is whether the lagging income groups, even if they are large, can contribute a significant amount of work to the national output. For example, if all income laggards are retired people upwards of 65 or 70, it is unlikely that they can contribute much to the size of the total national product, however severely they may feel the pinch of inflation.

All things considered, it seems unlikely that inflation will stimulate a large addition to the national output via this channel. In fact, as I shall argue below, the American economy has become to a larger extent than is generally realized an income-adjusting economy. Few major economic groups face serious income lags in moderate inflation, on the evidence of the past two decades. The largest groups pinched by inflation on income account are old folks and government-controlled employees, not likely sources of major increases in productive power. Except for the war period, the labor force (i.e., people in and looking for jobs) has shown no significant tendency to grow during inflation as a percentage of total population of labor force age. While the proportion of women holding jobs has risen steadily over the past quarter century, outside the war period there is no significant relationship between the rate of increase and the rate of inflation.

( (c) How about the argument that *expectation* of *continuing* inflation will lead to increased real output? This is an obviously short-run argument, applicable, if at all, in periods of unemployment. Then a shortage of demand keeps people unemployed, and anything that increases total spending may increase total employment and output. Evidence that expected price increases stimulate increased spending is reasonably plentiful, especially in business inventory speculation. There is some evidence, too, that consumers buy ahead on durables when they expect rising prices. But these are obviously temporary, short-lived phenomena) People and businesses can not be expected to pile up inventories indefinitely on speculation that prices tomorrow will be higher than today.

(4) One more possible effect of inflation on the level of total output requires attention, although its impact is at most a slow one. This is the effect on the rate of economic growth. ( Inflation may increase saving relative to current consumption, thereby shifting resources from producing current consumption goods to capital goods. This shift will have no effect on total current output (though it will reduce the level of current consumption), but as capital goods build up it will gradually increase the total output of future years. Conversely, inflation may discourage saving, thereby generating the reverse series of events and pulling long-run future output below its otherwise likely level.)

Historians have argued that over the centuries inflation has shifted income from the poor to the rich and from workers to businessmen. This, they argue, has increased the volume of saving and investment and speeded the rate of economic growth.[4] But while the preponderance of evidence seems to

[4] A leading statement is that of Professor Earl Hamilton, *op. cit.* See also the other references cited in footnote 1.

support this view, the case is by no means clear. Whatever the lesson of history, more recent experience throws grave doubt on this hypothesis. For, as is argued in the following sections, at least in the recent American inflation it is not true that the share of profits has increased relative to wages, nor that the share of the rich has increased. On balance, the wage share has risen appreciably relative to property income. Thus, the argument that inflation induces more saving and investment via this channel cannot be accepted if recent experience predicts the future.

A precisely counter argument has often been made—that inflation *discourages* saving and *retards* capital accumulation, because inflation erodes the value of accumulated savings and encourages current consumption. Here again, scattered supporting evidence is plentiful, and the case is convincing in hyper-inflations. But counter-examples are easy to find—for example, in almost all the post-World War II inflations of the western world when capital accumulation has proceeded very rapidly. More complete evidence on this issue is presented below. At the moment, it is sufficient to note that modern society provides some effective investment channels to escape the erosion of inflation, at least for sophisticated savers, and that in moderate inflation the force of this counter-savings effect is not very clear.

Inflation may stimulate investment, and hence the rate of economic growth, through other financial channels. For any quoted rate of interest borrowers must pay to obtain funds to finance real investment, inflation reduces the "actual" rate below the quoted rate. This is because each dollar of interest paid at the higher price level represents less "actual" cost. If, therefore, inflation does not force up quoted interest rates, it acts to reduce the real cost of borrowing and hence stimulates investment.) But experience in many countries suggests that quoted interest rates rise in inflation, thus partially (but generally not completely) negating this effect.

Inflation may also stimulate investment if it forces up the prices of equity securities relative to other prices. This will make it cheaper for firms to obtain equity funds for investment, and will tend to stimulate real investment. Experience suggests that sometimes this relative price shift has prevailed, other times not.

One last word on the evidence relating inflation to changes in total production and employment. Table 2 summarizes the experience of seven leading European countries plus the United

TABLE 2

INFLATION, PRODUCTION AND EMPLOYMENT, 1952–55[a]
(1952 = 100)

|  |  | U.S. | Bel-gium | France | Ger-many | Italy | Nether-lands | Sweden | U.K. |
|---|---|---|---|---|---|---|---|---|---|
| Cost of Living— | 1953 | 101 | 100 | 99 | 98 | 102 | 100 | 101 | 103 |
|  | 1954 | 101 | 102 | 99 | 98 | 105 | 104 | 102 | 105 |
|  | 1955 | 101 | 101 | 100 | 100 | 108 | 106 | 105 | 110 |
| Industrial Production— | 1953 | 108 | 100 | 97 | 109 | 110 | 110 | 100 | 106 |
|  | 1954 | 100 | 106 | 106 | 122 | 120 | 120 | 104 | 114 |
|  | 1955 | 112 | 114 | 117 | 141 | 130 | 128 | 110 | 119 |
| Employment— | 1953 | 103 | 99 | 98 | 104 | 100 | 103 | 97 | 101 |
|  | 1954 | 100 | 99 | 99 | 109 | 101 | 107 | 98 | 104 |
|  | 1955 | 102 | 101 | 100 | 118 | 103 | 109 | 100 | 107 |

[a] Data from H. Herbert Furth, *op. cit.*, pp. 336–337. All figures are annual averages, based on official governmental sources.

States over a recent mild inflationary period of 1952 through 1955. It shows no consistent relationship at all between inflation and changes in production. The largest increase in output and employment occurred in West Germany, which had no inflation at all; the smallest in Sweden which had an intermediate amount of inflation. Italy, with about the same price increase as Sweden and the United Kingdom, had a substantially larger increase in output than either. The United States and Belgium, with almost no inflation, had a bigger increase in output than mildly inflationary Sweden but less than non-inflationary Germany and the mildly inflationary Netherlands. Nor can the apparent failure of inflation to explain differing rates of growth in output be explained by introducing such other obvious inter-country differences as differential increases in the supply of money, differing money wage rates relative to prices, or differing positions on international trade account.[5]

In summary, the effect of moderate inflation on total real output appears to be slight under most circumstances, and *a priori* not predictable. Inflation generally does not reduce total output through the oft-claimed "disruption" of productive processes until something approaching severe hyper-inflation is reached. But neither is there much evidence that moderate inflation stimulates total output. Whether inflation generally produces an ensuing "bust" is a little less easy to answer. Clearly it may, in a sharp, speculation-based inflation. But equally clearly, moderate inflation need not lead to the oft-predicted bust. Overall, moderate inflation may have some effect in stimulating total real output in an underemployed economy. But the effect in the modern American scene of high level employment seems unlikely to be substantial in either direction.[6]

[5] For a more complete analysis of this period with the relevant data, see J. Herbert Furth, "Indicators of Inflation in Western Europe, 1952-1955," *Review of Economics and Statistics,* August, 1956.

[6] In the interest of brevity and simplicity, the international effects of inflation are omitted completely. For the United States as a whole this probably does not distort greatly the conclusions reached. For some sectors of the economy, however, the foreign trade repercussions might be dominant. And for most other countries, more heavily dependent on foreign trade, such an omission would not be tolerable.

## V[7]

If slow inflation hasn't recently had much effect on the size of the national income pie, does it alter the relative size of the pieces going to different individuals and economic groups? The answer is, if we can judge from the American inflation of the past two decades: Yes, but not as much as is often claimed. And the redistribution that does take place does not correspond very well to some of the common preconceptions about inflation.[8]

For example, over the 1939-52 period, when most of the recent American inflation was concentrated, just about everyone's real income went up. Total output in the economy nearly doubled. Within the rapidly growing total, wages did *not* lag

[7] The next four sections are based on a more complete analysis recently published elsewhere: G. L. Bach and A. Ando, "The Redistributional Effects of Inflation," *Review of Economics and Statistics,* February, 1957.

[8] Footnote for economists: In considering the redistributional effects of inflation, I have used the following four propositions as an analytical framework:

1. Inflation redistributes real purchasing power (over current output and over assets) from those whose incomes rise less rapidly relative to the prices they pay as a result of inflation to those whose incomes rise more rapidly relative to the prices they pay. More roughly: inflation redistributes real purchasing power from those whose incomes rise more slowly to those whose incomes rise more rapidly.

2. Inflation redistributes real purchasing power from those whose assets rise more slowly in price as a result of inflation to those whose assets rise more rapidly in price.

3. Inflation redistributes real purchasing power from creditors to debtors, when debts are stated in fixed dollar terms.

4. To the extent that accurate expectations of continuing inflation affect economic behavior, the redistributional effects indicated above will tend to be negated, except where readjustment of terms of economic contracts is prevented or retarded (by government rules, existence of long term contracts, unequal knowledge, unequal bargaining power, and so on).

behind profits as a share of the national income; on the contrary, the wage share grew over the period. Farmers, who are commonly supposed to gain most from inflation, saw their share of the national income decline persistently—perhaps in spite of the inflation, but decline nevertheless. Unincorporated

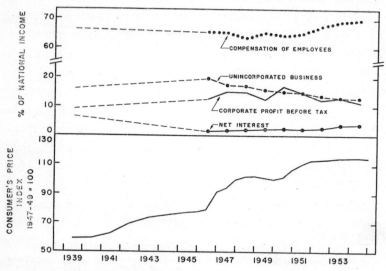

FIG. 1. SHARES OF NATIONAL INCOME IN INFLATION, 1939-54.

businesses, usually thought to be gainers from inflation, took a cut in their share. The interest share fell drastically during World War II, as interest rates were held down by government policy, but it has remained substantially unchanged since then. The rent share has changed little. Nor is there any evidence that inflation shifted income from the poor to the rich; if there was a small effect, it was probably the other way. Figure 1 pictures these changes, adding two years to indicate that no drastic reversals occurred after the price rise levelled off.

The shifting of relative income position among these major

economic groups was not great. But inflation had a drastic impact on particular individuals and sub-groups. Since inflation penalizes primarily those whose incomes rise more slowly than the incomes of their fellows, it was those on relatively fixed incomes who lost relatively, whether they were rich or poor, young or old, farmer or city-dweller.

Above all, it was older people whose piece of the national income pie apparently suffered most. Their share of the national income dropped substantially as inflation ate away at their largely fixed incomes, and their actual per capita *real* income may be little higher today than it was in 1939. Moreover, here it appears that inflation did discriminate against the middle incomes and the poor. Well-to-do retired individuals could afford to diversify the investments underlying their retirement incomes, and to include substantial amounts of such variable income assets as common stocks and real estate whose dollar yields increased with inflation. But to the lower or middle income family or widow this alternative was hardly open. Their only major hope for increased dollar income was from governmental social security, or going back to work.

The other most important lagging income group was teachers almost everywhere, and employees of governments and eleemosynary institutions generally—in some cases to such an extent that their real incomes have actually declined over two decades when average real income in the economy rose about 75 percent.

The fact that income shares changed generally in favor of private employees (wage and salary workers) and against non-business employees, old people, unincorporated businesses, and interest receivers during the long 1939-1952 American inflation does not, of course, prove that this shift was due to the inflation. Still less does it prove that a similar shift would be extended in any future inflation. But the observed facts do emphasize that the widely-held wage-lag hypothesis is highly questionable in modern America, as is the presumption that businesses generally gain from inflation. Neither was true during the period observed. If inflation pushed in the commonly supposed directions, its push was not strong enough to overcome other factors pushing toward the observed results. Looking ahead to one of my main theses in the following chapters, we live in a society where the major economic groups are increasingly effective in protecting their own income shares, and where private wage and salary earners are especially successful, at the expense of more passive, quasi-fixed income groups.

## VI

Thus far we have been looking at the impact of inflation on the size of the national income pie and on the size of the pieces into which the pie is divided. On neither score does moderate inflation appear to exercise as much impact as is often imagined. But inflation has another set of economic effects— effects on the distribution of *wealth*, as contrasted with the distribution of current income.

It is well known that inflation transfers wealth (future purchasing power) from creditors to debtors. This is so because the debtor who borrows $1000 and repays the same $1000 later when prices are twice as high repays only half as much real purchasing power. Thus, in effect, inflation has transferred $500 of wealth to him from the creditor. This effect occurs for all debtors vis-a-vis all creditors, wherever the debt is stated in a fixed number of dollars.

The American inflation from 1939 to 1952 wiped out in this way about half a trillion dollars of creditors' claims on debtors (in 1952 prices). All fixed dollar value intangible assets (such as bank deposits, currency, mortgages, government and corporation bonds, life insurance reserves, and pension and retirement funds) are debts owed to creditors that are susceptible to this erosion by inflation. In 1939, all such "monetary" assets, as I shall call them, totalled about $321 billion. If we calculate the loss of purchasing power on these debts up to 1952, and make a similar calculation for the additional debts of each following year, we obtain the *rough* $500 billion estimate of inflation's erosion of the real purchasing power of creditors over the period. By 1952, such monetary assets in the economy had risen to about $1 trillion, and in the years since then much higher, so the potential dollar loss of present creditors is far greater in the event of further inflation.

Who gained this half trillion dollars of purchasing power transferred from creditors to debtors during the inflation? To answer we need a sectorized picture of the economy, showing main debtor and creditor groups. This is provided by Table 3.

TABLE 3

NET DEBTORS AND CREDITORS IN THE AMERICAN ECONOMY, 1939–1949[a]
(In billions of dollars)

|  | 1939 | 1949 |
| --- | --- | --- |
| Households | +87 | +249 |
| Unincorporated Businesses | + 3 | + 16 |
| Non-financial Corporations | −25 | − 17 |
| Financial Corporations | − 3 | + 17 |
| Governments | −68 | −263 |

[a] Positive figure shows net creditor status; negative figure shows net debtor status. Data computed from Raymond Goldsmith, *A Study of Saving in the United States* (Princeton University Press, 1955 Vol. III, Tables W-14, 15, and 16.

In summary, the table shows that "households" (that is families and individuals) were massive net creditors. By 1950, their holdings of fixed-value monetary assets exceeded their debts to other groups in the economy by about $250 billion. The main offsetting debtor was the federal government, with a net outstanding debt of securities and currency of over $260 billion. Unincorporated businesses (farmers, professional men, small retailers, and so on) were moderate net creditors, while non-financial corporations (manufacturing, railroad, public utility, and other such companies) were roughly offsetting net debtors, at around $15 billion each in 1950. Although the 1939 figures were much smaller, roughly the same relative positions prevailed then, at the beginning of the period.

The picture is thus clear. Inflation caused a massive transfer of purchasing power from households, as the major net creditors, to the federal government, as the major net debtor. But this is clearly not the end of the matter, since the government is not some separate entity but is rather an agency for all of us. We must look *through* the government to see who are the actual beneficiaries of this inflation-induced levy on creditors.

At first blush, it would appear that taxpayers (that is, all of us in our capacities as taxpayers) are the gainers. We now need to give up less purchasing power in taxes to meet payments on interest and principal on the government debt because of inflation. Since government bondholders and taxpayers are not identical there is a real shift of wealth from creditors to taxpayers.

But it is highly unlikely that the federal debt will be paid off through taxation in the foreseeable future. Who then is the gainer from the purchasing power confiscated from government creditors by inflation? The answer is, the buying public as a whole, in proportion to its expenditures. Bondholders' real purchasing power is reduced, thereby increasing the share of total current output of goods and services that can be commanded by the rest of the buying public as their incomes rise with inflation. Put in common sense language, government bondholders and money-holders are partially expropriated by inflation, and the benefit is distributed over the whole population, with the biggest benefits to those who buy the most. Although government creditors and spenders are the same people to some extent, on balance savers *in fixed dollar value assets* subsidize spenders. There is no clear evidence that this effect transfers real income from the poor to the rich, or vice versa.[9]

## VII

Households are the overwhelming net creditors in the modern American economy. But all of us are parts of households, and more information on particular types of households is needed if we are to see clearly the impact of inflation on us as creditors. Fortunately, some data are now available to help assess this effect. The information is summarized in Table 4.

All households combined hold about 25 percent of their total wealth in the form of fixed dollar value ("monetary") assets. By contrast, they are in debt up to only a little over 10 percent of their total wealth. The difference is a measure of their net creditor position. Nearly every major group of households is a substantial net creditor. This is true for every income level, including very low ones. It is true of every major occupational group. It is true for every age group except those in the 25-34 age bracket who are just establishing households and families. It is true for families at every level of positive net worth—that is, where the family's total assets exceed its debts. The only two exceptions are some two million house-

[9] This analysis implicitly assumes a full employment economy. If unemployment prevails, the effect of inflation in reducing the real purchasing power of creditors may simply reduce their spending without stimulating any offsetting increase in the spending of others, thus providing a net deflationary force. The strength of this effect is uncertain with present ignorance as to the effect of liquid assets on current spending.

## TABLE 4

ASSETS AND DEBTS OF HOUSEHOLDS, EARLY
1950[a]

| | Per cent of all house-holds | Total assets ($ billion) | Per cent of total assets: | | |
|---|---|---|---|---|---|
| | | | Mone-tary assets | Variable price assets | Debts |
| All Households | 100 | 613 | 24 | 76 | 11 |
| *By 1949 money income before taxes:* | | | | | |
| Under $1,000 | 14 | 39 | 19 | 81 | 12 |
| 1,000–2,999 | 40 | 119 | 26 | 74 | 13 |
| 3,000–4,999 | 29 | 150 | 27 | 73 | 16 |
| 5,000–7,499 | 11 | 107 | 25 | 75 | 12 |
| 7,500 and over | 5 | 188 | 19 | 81 | 5 |
| *By Occupation:* | | | | | |
| Professional and semi-professional | 7 | 61 | 32 | 68 | 10 |
| Managerial | 4 | 40 | 27 | 73 | 12 |
| Self-employed | 8 | 155 | 16 | 84 | 6 |
| Clerical and skilled | 41 | 136 | 29 | 71 | 18 |
| Unskilled | 12 | 23 | 31 | 69 | 14 |
| Farm operator | 9 | 97 | 13 | 87 | 12 |
| Retired | 5 | 55 | 31 | 69 | 2 |
| All other | 14 | 46 | 28 | 72 | 8 |
| *By Net Worth in 1950:* | | | | | |
| Negative Net Worth | 5 | 2 | 30 | 70 | 490 |
| $0–1,999 | 33 | 17 | 46 | 54 | 33 |
| 2,000–9,999 | 34 | 117 | 29 | 71 | 20 |
| 10,000–24,999 | 18 | 162 | 24 | 76 | 9 |
| 25,000–59,999 | 7 | 135 | 22 | 78 | 6 |
| 60,000 and over | 3 | 180 | 17 | 83 | 3 |
| *By Age of Head of Household:* | | | | | |
| 18–24 | 10 | 9 | 23 | 77 | 20 |
| 25–34 | 23 | 69 | 22 | 78 | 27 |
| 35–54 | 40 | 285 | 24 | 76 | 12 |
| 55 and over | 26 | 244 | 23 | 77 | 4 |

[a] Data from Raymond Goldsmith, *A Study of Saving in the United States* (Princeton University Press, 1955), Tables W-46, 47, 48, 49, based in turn primarily on Federal Reserve-Michigan Survey Research Center survey of consumer finances for early 1950. Total households columns may not add to totals because of minor unascertained items and rounding.

Total assets and total net creditor position of households shown here are much smaller than in Table 3. This is because the Table 3 data are adjusted for substantial under-reporting in the Table 4 survey, and because Table 3 monetary assets include life insurance reserves, pension and retirement funds, currency holdings, and other intangible assets excluded from the Table 4 figures.

holds whose net worth is less than zero—that is, whose debts exceed their total assets of all sorts; and families in the 25-34 age bracket where many go heavily in debt to start families and to buy houses, home furnishings, and other durables.

But the extent to which different groups are net creditors varies a good deal. The heaviest net creditors, relative to their incomes, are older people, especially those who are retired. They hold a larger proportion of their wealth in fixed dollar value assets than do any other major group, largely because of the importance to them of insurance, and pension and other retirement funds. It is they who stand to lose most as creditors when inflation comes, relative to their incomes. Moreover, they are least in debt, to reap offsetting benefits on that score.

At the other extreme, the very penurious or injudicious who are so heavily in debt as to have a negative net worth, and younger families in the 25-34 age range, are the least susceptible to "creditor" loss from inflation. They are substantially in debt, which is, other things equal, a good thing to be during inflation.

The position of very well-to-do families is interesting, and mixed. Such families are slightly higher net creditors than the average (relative to their total wealth), and their debts are small. Thus, they appear quite vulnerable to inflation. But they hold an exceptionally large proportion of their total assets in "variable price" form (common stocks, real estate, and so on), which serves as a partial offset to their exposure as net creditors.

Strikingly, most American households appear to have made comparatively little effort during the long period of persistent inflation to switch from their position as heavy net creditors. While the data are inadequate, they suggest only a mild attempt by households to shift to more "inflation-proof" assets, even in periods of rapidly rising prices. This contrasts with their behavior as earners, where employees generally appear to have been both sensitive to inflation and effective in maintaining or improving their income shares during inflationary periods.

## VIII

Lastly, I should like to take a very brief look at the position of business corporations in inflation. Economists have generally written of non-financial corporations as heavy net debtors, likely to gain substantially on that account in any inflation period. The fact is that over the past two decades non-financial corporations in the aggregate have been net debtors, but only to a small extent. Moreover, as many as a third of such corporations have been net creditors at any given time during this period; many have shifted back and forth from one status to the other.

Thus for business corporations in the mass, gain from a net debtor status cannot be counted on to yield big benefits in inflation. For most companies, other factors play dominant roles in determining the economic well-being of the corporation —especially sales volume and increases in current costs relative to selling prices. Investigation of a carefully chosen sample of about fifty American corporations from 1939 to 1952 revealed little direct relationship between net debtor or creditor position and how profitable they were or how highly valued their common stocks were in the market. On the other hand, growth in sales volume appeared to explain much of the difference in profitability among the companies. Tests for the importance of wage increases relative to price increases, though extremely difficult to make, suggest that this factor may account for much of the rest of the differences among company performances.[10]

On income account, the reported corporate profit share in the national income remained roughly stable during the long American inflation, lagging behind the wage and salary share. Actually, these figures, reported above, paint the picture too bright for corporations. Most American corporations charge depreciation on their plant and equipment on the basis of the actual (historical) cost of the assets, but replacement costs have risen steadily during the inflation. Thus, depreciation charges in inflation are consistently too small actually to replace the depreciated equipment. Similarly inventory accounting generally charges materials into costs at their original cost, even though in inflation they can be replaced only at higher prices. "Lifo" accounting partially remedies this under-costing, but only partially and many firms do not use the "Lifo" method. Put in other words, in inflation present accounting methods make reported profits look higher than they "really" are by the amount to which the depreciation and inventory costs charged fall short of actually replacing the assets and materials used up.

This is not a minor factor in rapid inflation. A recent study, sponsored by the American Accounting Association, suggested that such undercharging of real depreciation and inventory costs between 1940 and 1952 was enough to eat up nearly half of all reported profits in a small sample of diverse companies studied. If you remember that approximately half of all reported corporate profits are paid to the

[10] For details of this investigation, see Bach and Ando, *op cit.*, pp. 9-12.

federal government in income taxes, this means that actually income taxes took well over half of all "real" profits for this sample of companies, while inflation also ate up the purchasing power of nearly half of the remaining reported money profits.[11]

(While this finding may be extreme, it is clear that reported corporation profits during the inflation were substantially higher than was merited by the facts of replacement costs. Thus, *actual* corporate profits clearly failed to retain a stable share of the national income pie.) And the same over-reporting of profits would apply to many unincorporated businesses.

## IX

I have tried to summarize in this chapter—objectively and without evaluation—some of the major effects of moderate inflation on an economy like ours. Clearly the pattern is not simple, nor does careful examination bear out many widely held preconceptions.

( On the whole the effects appear to be less drastic than is often claimed. But they are by no means unimportant. Clearest of all, inflation has militated against savers—even savings in the form of corporate stocks, but especially savings held in fixed money value assets; against old folks; against employees of governments and eleemosynary institutions; and against unincorporated businesses.

[11] See Ralph C. Jones, *Price Level Changes and Financial Statements: Case Studies of Four Companies* (American Accounting Association, 1955). These calculations do not take into account the effect of inflation on the intangible assets and liabilities of the corporations. For a rough calculation of the effect of inflation during 1946 through 1951 on all American non-financial corporations which arrives at similar results, see D. A. Ferguson, "Accounting and the Price Level," *The Accounting Review,* October, 1954, p. 641. Calculations for a later period are presented by George Terborgh, *Corporate Profits in the Decade 1947-1956* (Machinery and Allied Products Institute, 1957).

Perhaps we should conclude from this survey that inflation is far less evil than it is often painted, and that we need not be concerned with avoiding it.) Perhaps the conclusion should be quite the contrary. The next chapter looks ahead at the prospects for inflation over the foreseeable future. Then I propose to drop my own cloak of ethical and economic neutrality, and to examine in detail the intermix of economic, ethical and political issues we face in determining the goals of social policy concerning inflation over the years ahead. We need to analyze these prospects carefully. (For inflation comes not from heaven but from the policies of men, and there is much we can do to affect its speed and to channel its differential effects on different groups, if we wish to do so.)

# 11 The Prospect Ahead

In Chapter I, I tried to paint a broad picture of the major economic effects of inflation in the United States over the past two decades. In this chapter, I shall have two major theses:

First, there will be persistent inflationary pressure in the United States over the foreseeable future.

Second, the roots of this pressure lie deep in our basic democratic political and social processes, as well as in our particular economic institutions, and this fact will make effective prevention of inflation unlikely, although there may well be intermittent periods of stable or even falling prices.

## I

Inflation, it is often said, is too much money chasing too few goods. This is a crude statement, but it has a strong element of truth. More precisely, inflationary pressure occurs when there is excess total demand for goods and services offered for sale at prevailing prices. Without this situation, substantial inflation will not continue. Though costs may "push" upward on prices, unless demand is growing the resultant price increases will not go very far. If we want to predict inflationary pressures in the future, therefore, we need to look at the likely level of total spending against the likely level of total goods and services available for purchase (what I have called the total pie, or the real national income or gross national product).[1]

Will total spending persistently run ahead of the real gross national product available over the years ahead, as I propose to argue? A brief look backward may help to provide perspective.

Inflation has vexed nations and their rulers since the earliest days of recorded history. In ancient times, little of man's livelihood passed through the market place, and inflation had only a limited import. Over the past few hundred years, however, increasing specialization, division of labor, and exchange have channelled more and more of the goods and services of the western world through the market. Thus, rising prices affect directly ever more people. And, as I indicated above, every major industrialized nation of the western world has faced inflation repeatedly over the past two centuries. In some nations there have been long valleys between the steep peaks of inflation, and there is a striking coincidence between wars and rising prices. But in every country, the net result over the decades has been a persistent uptrend of prices. Indeed, as I suggested at the outset, the amazing thing is that man has not long since come to expect inflation as the normal event and a continuing stable value of his monetary unit the exception.

[1] For more complete, but relatively non-technical, accounts of the major causes and courses of inflation, see "Inflation," *Encyclopaedia Britannica* (1955 and later editions); *The Course and Control of Inflation* (League of Nations, 1946); A. G. Hart, *Money, Debt, and Economic Activity* (Prentice Hall, 1953), Chapters 15 and 16; Lester V. Chandler, *Inflation in the United States, 1940-1948* (Harper and Brothers, 1951); and *The Economist* (London), August 18, 1951.

How have we done in the United States? Better than most. Each war or its aftermath has seen a huge peak of inflation—the 1780's, 1815, 1865, 1919-20, and 1948-51. War needs have diverted goods and men from civilian production, and new money has been created to pay for huge war outlays, rather than levying sufficient taxes to pay the bills. But in between these peaks, prices have dropped back toward, or even below, prewar levels. In the 1930's, for example, prices were little if any higher than a century before. And during the last third of the 19th century, a persistent downdrift of prices carried them below their bottoms of the preceding century. Except in war, the prodigious productivity of the expanding American economy has made it hard for inflation to get a toehold. Though total spending has risen decade after decade, the goods and services poured out into the market have risen apace. At least until the post-World War II period, the history of the American economy provides little support for the fear of inflation, except in connection with war.

In spite of this fact, I wish to argue that inflation will be a persistent force over the decades ahead—indeed, that we are already well into this long-range inflationary drift today, though this fact has been temporarily obscured by the special decline in farm prices over the past decade. Not that prices will rise every year and all the time. They certainly may not. Temporary setbacks of as much as two or three years may indeed occur. But these setbacks will be temporary and fewer than most people suppose, and the general trend will be clearly and persistently upward. If it does not amount to more than two or three percent per year on the average, those who fear inflation can count themselves fortunate. On the other hand, short of war there are strong forces to check inflation far short of the post-war runaway price increases which we have all read about in the defeated nations of central Europe and Asia.

## II

What has happened to so increase the likelihood of persistent inflation in America, while still keeping price increases far short of real runaway inflation levels? Surely not the failure of the vaunted American productivity to pour goods and services out onto the market. There is every indication that the economy's performance has steadily improved on this score, and no visible reason why the full-employment capacity of the economy will not continue to grow at at least the same rate that has prevailed over past decades—around 3 percent per annum, as a rough approximation. It seems to me, indeed, that a good presumption can be built up for an even more rapid rate—nearer 4 than 3 percent. And over a decade an extra percent per annum means an extra $50 billion or so of additional total output. This spectacular increase in potential real output is one of the main reasons we can expect that peacetime inflation will not reach beyond modest proportions.

But why inflation at all in the face of this huge increase of goods and services available for purchase—an additional $15 billion or so per year on top of the already huge gross national product of around $425 billion annually? I suggest six major reasons which, in combination, seem to me to present a formidable presumption.

### (1) The Sanctity of "Full Employment"

In the United States, and indeed in all of the western world, maintenance of high level employment has become not only *a* goal, but *the main* goal, of economic policy. Republican and Democrat alike, liberal and conservative, employer and employee—all are agreed that above all we must avoid another major depression like that of the 1930's, with its millions of desolate unemployed, its never-ending breadlines, its cold grey desperation and mass waste of men and machines.

Here and there, a voice is raised that maybe a little unemployment would be a good thing. But no one in a position of responsibility, governmental or otherwise, dares to urge this openly. Political responsibility burns deeply and quickly develops a profound concern with keeping the spectre of unemployment under tight control—and understandably so. It is true that a whole generation of young workers is now coming on the political and economic scene who have never known mass unemployment and the gripping fear of hunger and desolation bred of the 1930's. But in their minds the *right* to a job has supplanted the fear of unemployment in their fathers'— and the result is the same in both cases. Unemployment must not, and, in the minds of the younger generation at least, need not be tolerated.

Is this picture of the sacrosanctity of full employment overdone—a will-of-the-wisp I have conjured up? I think not. The evidence of political and economic behavior seems to me clear. No party in power or out can seriously contemplate inaction when unemployment mounts. Unemployment above moderate "frictional" levels has stirred both parties to vigorous action, and to strong assurances of willingness to move quickly to whatever action may be required to avoid mass layoffs. On this score Mr. Eisenhower and Mr. Stevenson have been markedly similar, and so has the behavior of the stalwarts of their respective political parties, the occasional pronouncements of such figures as Secretary Humphrey and Senator Byrd notwithstanding.

## (2) *The (Apparent) World War II Demonstration that Massive Government Spending Can Produce Full Employment*

World War II showed vividly the power of government spending—when it is big enough and when it is financed largely by deficits—to put millions of unemployed people back to work. What all the efforts of the New Deal could not manage in the 1930's, massive war spending accomplished in record time in the early 1940's. By late 1941, unemployment had vanished. While it would be naive to argue that government spending alone was responsible for this abrupt end to the long stagnation in the 1930's, it would be equally naive not to recognize the central role played by such spending.

This lesson, following the Keynesian revolution in economic thought of the 1930's and the desperate struggle against mass unemployment during those years, was learned, perhaps too well, by economists, by government officials, by labor leaders and their followers, and even by many businessmen. In many cases, the learning was almost subconscious, and often over the bitter resistance of previous training in fiscal and financial orthodoxy. But consciously or subconsciously, the lesson was learned. By spending enough, the government can put unemployed men back to work and keep them there—not just a few men, but millions of them. The later consequences may be painful, or even terrible. But government spending can put men back to work, if that is the first objective.

It was this realization, I believe, that made the sanctity of full employment thinkable. If unemployment can be conquered, then it is thinkable to give this goal first place in economic action—for economists, for politicians, for workers, and for businessmen. For a generation that suffered through the desolation of the 'thirties, there was now a chance to be rid of its greatest disaster, even if the bankers and the business-men cried out against government spending. For a generation maturing through the war and postwar years, why should unemployment be tolerated? History, the history of the past two decades, shows clearly that unemployment *need* not be tolerated. Aspirations, like politics, are the art of the possible. Substantially full employment has become a reasonable goal.

(3) *The Increasing Political and Economic Strength of Major Socio-economic Groups and the Increasingly "Adminis-tered" Structure of Prices in the Economy*

The third force increasing the likelihood of inflation is the increasing political and economic strength of major socio-economic groups and the increasingly "administered" struc-ture of prices in the American economy. There has been a persistent, though not steady, tendency in all democratic countries for trade unions to become stronger. This means an increasingly powerful upward push on wages, the major com-ponent of costs in the modern economy. But equally impor-tant, as economists discovered a quarter century ago, most other prices in the American economy are no longer estab-lished impersonally in highly competitive markets. Instead, they are "administered"—set by leading firms, and by bar-gains between leading buyers and sellers. Often these bargains are closely constrained by the competitive pressure of the market, but administered the prices and wages are, none-theless.[2] Many services are priced in this way.

[2] In an article published after these lectures were given, Professor J. K. Galbraith has spelled this point out in detail, providing an integrated analysis of the role of differentially administered prices in the inflationary process. See "Market Structure and Stabilization Policy," *Review of Economics and Statistics*, May, 1957, especially pages 124-132.

Most significant of all, important economic groups have discovered their power through the political process to achieve goals they cannot achieve satisfactorily through the market place. If farmers cannot get higher prices through the free market, they can through Congress. If workers cannot get livable wages through the market, they can bring great pressure on their governments, directly and by swaying public opinion, for higher minimum wages. If businessmen cannot get high enough prices through the market for coal or milk, they can get help from Washington or the local state capitol.

The import of this discovery is far-reaching. For with this recognition sellers need not be content with what the market gives them, even though individually they may be very small sellers indeed. A century, or even a half century ago, the decision of the market was inexorable, except under most exceptional circumstances. This is no longer true. What the market hath made, Congress can amend. Congress intervenes in many ways, direct and devious. And the pressures on Congress to act in these ways will be very strong indeed if the outcome of the market is not satisfactory to the major socio-economic groups and individuals in the market.

(4) *The Trend to the Left, and Increased Government Responsibility for the Welfare of the Masses*

The century of the common man is no time for deflation. Deflation is essentially undemocratic—it obviously takes something away from many people. On the contrary, modern democracy is established to maximize the responsiveness of the government to the common man and to his wants.

It is significant that in England the return of the Conservatives to power in 1951 brought little overthrow of the welfare state innovations of Labor. Here it is perhaps equally significant that the Eisenhower Administration has shown little enthusiasm for a real return to pre-New Deal days, and little ability to throw out the fundamental New Deal social benefits on those few occasions when it has tried. Nor is it insignificant that President Eisenhower, for all his vast personal popularity, was unable in 1956 to pull in a Republican majority in either branch of Congress.

The United States today is far from the welfare state of the United Kingdom, with its cradle-to-the-grave program of government benevolence for the little man. But it is far also from the United States of the 1920's, with little sign of returning. The economic group in trouble, especially if it is a group of the "little men," can turn to the government for help with a reasonable expectation that it will not go away empty-handed. And help costs money, through government expenditures or through higher prices to the consumer produced indirectly by government policies.

Democratic governments, as the London *Economist* has trenchantly pointed out, will always *tend* toward spending more and taxing less. They will always tend to underestimate the inflationary forces at work during an inflation, and to accept the more optimistic of two estimates being put forward. If they do not, they will be replaced before long with governments that do.

### (5) *War—Hot War and Cold War*

The fifth force pushing toward more inflation is war—hot war and cold. War—hot or cold—is immensely expensive. Modern history shows no war that has not brought inflation. This is even truer today than in the past, because of the fantastic cost of preparing for, fighting, and cleaning up after modern war. If we become engaged in even luke-warm war—in minor skirmishes—the potential price increase is huge. With only continuation of the cold war, the drain on the public purse is enormous, requiring a painful and ill-received mass of taxation to keep the federal budget balanced. Government spending of this magnitude for an "unproductive" purpose cannot avoid pushing upward on prices in a democratic society.

## (6) *The End of the Gold Standard*

The sixth factor underlying the prospect for inflation is the end of gold standard. It is now a quarter century since the late gold standard went to its generally unlamented death. Surely the gold standard had many failings, and I would not want to see it back. But with all its failings, it did provide a monetary "religion" that brought the government and the public up short when they felt the urge to spend more than they were taking in, both through the check it imposed on expansion of the money supply to finance new spending and through the international gold drain if inflation exceeded the rate in other countries. Today the gold standard, fair weather friend that it was, is gone, and we have nothing to put in its place save our own resolution. Perhaps a modern-day equivalent of those gold standard watchdogs, the international bankers, would make us squirm more when we contemplate the inflationary consequences of our policies. But none such looms up on the horizon—nor do we really show signs of wanting one.

This concatenation of factors creates in the American democratic society a strong presumption of persistent inflationary pressure. Put together these six points. We are committed to maintaining substantially full employment. Economists, government officials, labor leaders, businessmen, and, most important of all, the common man are all convinced, or at least suspect strongly, that government spending can produce high level employment—even though the spending program implied by this belief makes many of these same people extremely uncomfortable. A more sophisticated few understand that the same result may be obtained without increased expenditures merely by lowering taxes.

With most important prices in the economy made on a bargaining or administered basis by large organizations and economic power groups, price-setting can and does reflect the views and judgments of the price-makers. And these large organizations and power groups increasingly recognize the power they have through the political process to achieve what they may not be able to accomplish unaided in the market place. The end of monetary expansion imposed by the government or by gold could put a monetary ceiling on prices, forcing employers to resist more vigorously the wage demands of their unions. But if the unions and businessmen can, instead, count on the government to add enough spending power to maintain sales and full employment even at higher prices, little wonder that they push wages and prices steadily upward in search of larger income shares for themselves. What have they to lose?

It is important to recognize that this process is by no means confined to wage bargains followed by price increases, nor is it limited solely to big unions and big businesses. So long as income groups feel confident that total demand will be continually expanded to bail out any substantial over-pricing of goods or labor in the economy, they need not even be powerful price setters themselves or effective political pressure units to be reasonably secure in pushing up wages and prices. The big, powerful, visible price-setter, such as the United Auto Workers or U. S. Steel, can feel secure that large-scale unemployment generated in its industry will be an immediate cause of widespread concern, and of reasonably prompt government remedial action. This is especially true since it is a price-setter for a much wider sector of the economy and similar increases can be expected to follow there without undue delay. The little union or little firm must worry much more lest it simply price itself out of a market, and it dare not get far ahead of the parade. But for a groupistic economy, the pattern of wage and price behavior, though far from simple and orderly, is sufficiently clear to permit most sellers to judge reasonably well how far and how fast they can safely go in relation to the leaders.

The tendency of businesses to raise prices is further increased by their growing emphasis on obtaining funds for expansion through retained earnings rather than in the open markets. When management refuses to dilute the ownership of its stockholders by raising funds through new ownership shares, the pressure to increase profits is intensified correspondingly. Profits must provide both adequate dividends and funds to expand in a rapidly growing economy. When costs rise, prices must rise more than apace to provide the funds needed for these parallel purposes.

To this general picture, we must add the pervasive attitude that the government needs to "take care" of economic groups which fall behind in the competitive struggle for one reason or another—farmers, coal miners, New England mill towns, the children and the aged. If we take care of these, is it unreasonable for the solid, hardworking groups to expect and obtain substantial pay increases? And can we object if businesses raise prices when their costs creep steadily upward? Is not "live and let live" the right attitude for a democratic nation? On the one hand, benefits for the "needy" cost money—increasing the persistent tendency toward an unbalanced budget. On the other hand, they weaken the moral and operational position of the government in fighting undue wage and price increases by those who pay the bills.

In the gold standard days there was a ceiling on all this. When bank reserves were used up and no more gold was available, tight money laid its cold hand on the boom. Even without the gold standard, the monetary and fiscal authorities today can play this same role of limiting the inflationary up-sweep of wages and prices, *if* the government does not feel obliged to assure high level employment. But a government committed in substance to full employment is no longer *the* authority in the economy establishing the level of income, employment and prices. Organized labor, business, agriculture —these and the other major economic groups in the economy have power comparable to that of the government itself. If they insist on claiming more income through pushing up wages and prices, the government has no real alternative but to increase government spending and the money supply to support employment at the higher costs and prices.

Probably the government can guarantee full employment, but it cannot guarantee full employment without inflation. On the contrary, in explicitly or implicitly guaranteeing high level employment it comes dangerously close by the same act to guaranteeing inflation. The price level becomes indeterminate, governed by a kind of trilateral bargaining among wage setters, price setters, and the government. This bargaining has a strong presumption of inflation, as money-income disputes are adjudicated upward at the expense of the "non-active," fixed incomes in society. And the confusion over the real effects of inflation, coupled with the present diffused economic responsibilities in government, provides an ideal opportunity for powerful income groups to advance their own interests without ever exposing the real issues to the public gaze.

The crux of the matter is that in such a world the central issue of income distribution is shifted from the impersonal market place to the combined bargaining processes of the market *and* the halls of Washington—to an arena where the governmental monetary-fiscal authorities are only one of the powerful "authorities." As long as none of the major non-governmental groups believes that the government will bail out unemployment and falling sales by expansionary monetary-fiscal policy, the fear of going too far and inducing unemployment and lower sales serves as a major moderating force on the struggle for income position and power. This has clearly been an important restraint over most of our history to date. But today this barrier may be perilously near to gone. In the modern democracy, it would be a remarkably insulated and politically insensitive government that would consistently permit the development of unemployment rather than expand purchasing power (and raise prices) to maintain total output and employment.

The logical result of my argument is alarming indeed. For in such a world, what limit is there on the inflationary spiral? In such a spiral, will not groups soon begin to anticipate the responses of the other groups and of the government itself, increasing their own income demands accordingly? In such a world the plight of the government may be an unhappy one indeed—try to keep *apace* with the ever-rising income demands of unions, businesses and farmers, or to lag just a little behind to slow the spiral—but never too far behind lest unemployment pile up nor too far ahead lest the inflationary spiral be further speeded.

## III

In spite of the logic of the above argument, such a runaway inflationary spiral in the United States seems to me extremely unlikely. There are four main reasons why.

The first is that people don't yet understand what they can get away with. While the preceding analysis would be far from novel to some union leaders, some farmers, and some businessmen, it would probably be amazing indeed to the mass of the American public—that any major income group can safely demand a continually rising income share, and get it, to at least a limited extent, so long as the government underwrites full employment and there are some fixed income groups left for inflation to squeeze out. But this ignorance can hardly be expected to continue indefinitely, and complete understanding is not necessary for the process to work reasonably well.

The second, closely related, reason is the pervasive force of competition. The individual business man always fears most the loss of customers to his competitors. Before he raises a price, he thinks long and hard unless he is sure his competitors will do likewise. And his competitors may be outside the industry in which he resides. Alcoa must be concerned with the relationship of its prices to those of copper and steel, as well as to the prices set by Reynolds and Kaiser Aluminum. Thus, although the business man may understand the final responsibility of the government monetary-fiscal policy to provide adequate total monetary demand for full employment, his immediate concern is for his competitive position, and he will resist wage pressures long and hard if they would force him to break the pattern of the competitive price structure within which he operates.

The third reason is the prodigious American productivity, on which I commented above. The American economy pours out ever more goods and services at a rate to match even a rapid rise in total spending—to put it another way, to offset even a rapid rise in the income claims of major economic groups. But this alone would not be enough either, for there is nothing to keep income groups from raising their claims even faster as they learn how fast productivity grows.

The fourth reason is at once the most tenuous and most powerful. It is the pervasiveness and persistence of strong stable money mores, even among many who suspect they may personally gain from "a little" inflation.

There is little evidence that the American public is much worried about moderate inflation, of say a few percent a year, at least unless it proceeds for several years. But there is much evidence that it views as a major, though dimly understood, calamity real galloping inflation like that of central Europe after World War I. Every American schoolboy seems to hear of the German people needing a wheelbarrow full of marks to buy a loaf of bread. The American man-in-the-street, that mythical individual, seems clearly in favor of a better standard of living and higher wages, and even profits, for everybody except ne'er-do-wells, and maybe a few of his special antagonists. But at the same time he is terribly afraid of runaway inflation, which he dimly associates with economic disruption and collapse and with poverty for the working man.

Thus, if my picture is correct, he is little inclined to criticize his neighbors, or even the economic royalists, for their attempts to improve their economic lots within reason. But he will be strongly opposed to any group that blatantly and obviously brings on drastic inflation. And he will be alarmed indeed should a rapid spiral of wage-price increases get under way, at say a rate of 10 or 20 percent a year, still a modest figure in comparison with the debacles he fears.

If this analysis is correct, widespread public support will develop for strong measures to stop any rapid peacetime inflation induced by spiraling income share claims and supported by expansionary monetary fiscal policy. In such a case, the essence of the inflationary process would be widely seen, and the authority of the government to resist inflationary income claims would be strengthened by this public support. I do not argue that such widespread anti-inflation support would necessarily be economically rational for all groups concerned, but merely that the support would come and that this fact drastically limits the possibility of rapid "pressure group" inflation in our society. You will recognize, of course, that my judgment of the public temper may be wrong, or that if I am right today that temper may change in the future. If that is the case, the possibility of really drastic inflation becomes ever more real as awareness grows of the implications of a substantially full employment guarantee.

## IV

A brief summary, then, on the prospects for inflation over the years ahead as they emerge from this analysis. I see a persistent inflationary bias, with prices and wages generally being pushed up faster than is consistent with full employment at stable prices—but with intermittent periods of weakness in output, production and prices as the economy grows unevenly.

The recession is far from an extinct dodo in our society. Social forecasting is a dangerous undertaking, but the probability seems strong of both secular inflation and intermittent recessions.

This persistent inflationary bias is already much in evidence, in spite of the widely noted stability of the consumer price level over the 1951-56 period. This performance was, indeed, somewhat encouraging. But a look into the price structure shows that over the period business, industrial and service prices drifted upward as average wages rose faster than average productivity, while farm prices fell so far that they held the over-all average of prices almost stable. But the decline in farm prices over the period was attributable mainly to the special weak position of agriculture in the economy. And while this position may not change much for many years ahead, it is clear that farm prices cannot continue their rapid decline, even though they may not go back up very much. If they merely stabilize around their present levels, this would remove the main force holding down the price average, and the price index will begin to rise apace with the updrift in non-agricultural prices. If farm prices should recoup some of their loss, then inflation will appear even more clearly. And this is precisely what happened in 1956 and 1957. Farm prices levelled off and turned upward slightly, while industrial prices continued their pronounced updrift. Result: a rise of 3 percent in the consumer goods price level in less than a year. Many years to come may look not much different.

# III   The Goals of Social Policy

THE PROSPECT is for secular inflation—not with certainty but with a strong probability. In the light of what we know about the economic effects of recent moderate inflation on the American economy, what are the implications of this prospect for the formation of governmental economic policy?

## I

High level employment without inflation is widely accepted as the proximate goal of economic stabilization policy. Substantially full employment can hardly be questioned as a major goal of economic policy in America, indeed in all the western democracies today. But substantial stability of the price level, important though it may be in many minds, is clearly at a different level in the means-ends schema of stabilization policy.

In the end, I suppose we all want the maximum of happiness or satisfaction. But converting this goal to an operational basis poses some sticky problems. While we are reasonably safe in putting the full employment goal near the top of the list, stable prices must be evaluated more as means toward achievement of more basic ends. Anyone who has thought much about the entire means-ends schema in economics knows how fast such analysis is drawn into the depths, or heights, of ethics and philosophy. Because I am not a philosopher, I shall arbitrarily draw the line at a set of what would generally be called "economic"goals, though the line is very hard indeed to draw.

How important an economic goal should price level stability (that is, avoidance of inflation) be for America today? To answer the question, I propose to investigate briefly five subsidiary questions, using the evidence of Chapter 1 wherever possible to throw light on the answers.

(1) Would price level stability contribute more to maintenance of substantially full employment than would alternative price level policies?
(2) Would price level stability contribute more than alternative policies to attaining the desired rate of economic growth?
(3) Would price level stability contribute most to effective allocation of economic resources?
(4) Would price level stability be more "equitable" than alternative price level policies?
(5) Lastly, would price level stability contribute most to producing a workable, viable socio-politico-economic society?

## II

(1) Would price level stability contribute more to maintenance of high level employment than would alternative price level policies? It depends . . . ! Let us begin by limiting the alternatives under consideration. Rule out deflation (that is, falling price levels) as an undesirable policy goal. And rule out drastic inflation (say more than 5 percent or so per year). What we are then asking is whether price level stability or moderately rising prices will contribute more toward continuing full employment.

If I draw a lesson from the analysis of Chapter 1, it is that under conditions like those in the United States since World War II it doesn't matter a lot one way or the other. We found little evidence that mild inflation reduced the size of the current gross national product—that is, kept employment below full levels. But neither was there much evidence that it stimualted higher employment and a larger real gross national product. The old presumption that inflation generates larger profits and hence larger investment and more employment was not borne out, since the basic wage-lag did not exist. While paper profits were expanded by under-charging of depreciation and of inventory costs, even then reported profits barely held their own and real profits clearly declined as a share of total national income. Nor, lastly, does the recent inflation suggest that moderate inflation leads strongly toward a "bust" following the inflationary "boom."

The analytically critical variables were suggested in Chapter 1. Increased spending on goods and services will always push toward more employment. When widespread unemployment exists this push is apt to be direct and effective; in a substantially fully employed economy the upward effect will be primarily on prices rather than on employment. Inflation may increase total spending and thus push upward on employment through two major channels.

First, inflation decreases the attractiveness of holding money as against spending it. But whether the increased spending will be on currently produced goods and services, on existing capital assets (such as used automobiles, existing houses, and the like), or on securities, is far from certain. And only if the spending is for currently produced goods and services will it directly stimulate employment. Inflation militates against saving in any form, but primarily against saving in the form of money or fixed-money-return assets such as bonds. The urge to avoid inflation's obvious erosion of the value of money may lead merely to transfer of saving in other forms, such as common stocks or real estate, although it probably also stimulates current consumption and investment spending to some extent in most cases.

Second, inflation may increase total spending and employ-ment if it raises selling prices generally faster than costs (which stimulates more output), and if it raises other costs faster than wages (which further induces the substitution of labor for other productive resources). This two-stage effect through changes in *relative* prices hinges largely on two factors: the differential inflation expectations of different individuals and economic groups; and the extent to which these expectations affect their respective behaviors.

*If* inflation is equally foreseen by all economic groups *and if* all are equally able to adjust their economic behavior to take this into account, there is little reason to expect relative prices, relative income shares, or the level of employment to change. But in fact, of course, people are not equally fitted to judge the likelihood of inflation, nor are they equally situated to adjust their economic behavior accordingly. Some groups have more effective access to the relevant information and a better basis for forming reasonable judgments about the likelihood of inflation than do others. Even more clearly, some groups simply cannot adjust their economic behavior quickly to ex-pected inflation. At the extreme are individuals and institutions completely removed from active participation in the economic process. There are the largely "passive"—retired persons, el-eemosynary institutions, those who live on charity. They have no prices they can raise to protect against the higher prices they must pay. Others operate on long-term fixed contracts—long-term lenders and landlords are major examples. Many others are bound by shorter-term fixed contracts—salaried employees, wage earners, and so on. At the other extreme,

speculators buy and sell on extremely short term with high flexibility.

Differential expectations and differential ability to adjust economically to these expectations produce changes in relative prices and income shares, and probably changes in employment. But the longer inflation is anticipated, the more groups in society are able to adjust the economic bargains they make. What we apparently saw in America over the past twenty years was a much larger amount of such adjustment than had seemed likely *a priori,* especially adjustments by the major laboring group. So recent history does not suggest that inflation leads to higher real output through the wage and other cost lag. And analytically, long-continued inflation seems ever less likely to have this effect.

(2) Would stable prices contribute more than alternative price level policies to attaining the desired rate of economic growth? Again, it depends . . . on the desired rate of growth, and on much the same factors considered just above.

How fast the economy should grow is a complex matter, but in the end it comes down largely to a value choice between larger consumption now versus larger consumption in the future. If we save more, we consume less now, but the productive capacity of the economy will grow faster and we can consume more in years to come. This is the basic choice facing a full employment economy.

Inflation may stimulate more rapid growth by increasing investment relative to consumption—that is, by directly transferring resources from producing goods for current consumption to producing machinery, plant, equipment and other capital goods that will increase total output in the future. Or inflation may stimulate more rapid growth indirectly by increasing saving relative to consumption spending, so that more saving in turn stimulates the increased investment in the preceding sentence. Conversely, inflation may retard the rate of growth by stimulating current consumption relative to saving and investment.

Which is the major effect of inflation? The answer, for moderate inflation of the recent American sort, is that nobody knows for sure. Most of the evidence summarized in Chapter 1 suggests that it probably doesn't make much difference either way. With the traditional wage-lage, it was generally argued that inflation stimulated profits and investment at the expense of current consumption, thereby speeding the rate of economic growth. But the importance of the effect was challenged even under those conditions. Today, if the wage lag does not occur —more generally, if the expectations adjustment process is pervasive—there is little reason to expect inflation-generated profits which will in turn pull resources from consumption to investment.

Indeed, if inflation expectations become strong and pervasive, they seem more likely to *reduce* current saving. Under inflation many forms of saving (such as bonds and money) are obviously eroded in real value, and few completely escape erosion. Inflation does not necessarily discriminate against savers, but it does force a discriminating investment policy for savings if their real value is to be preserved. Overall, though, this effect probably isn't strong enough or sure enough to provide much of a guide as to how strong a position we should take against mild inflation.

(3) Would price level stability contribute most to effective allocation of resources, following the preferences of consumers?[1] The answer is that price level stability is probably a little

---

[1] This leaves aside the division of resources between investment and consumption, which is covered by the preceding question.

better than slowly rising prices. But again, it depends . . . !

The advantage of a stable value of money lies primarily in the simpler basis it provides for expectations and planning. If the value of the monetary unit is stable, presumably consumers, businessmen and workers all make their economic decisions with a minimum of confusion due to uncertainty and ignorance about shifting prices resulting merely from changes in the value of money. If, as seems inevitably true, inflation brings some relative price changes, the allocation of resources is shifted somewhat in inflation from that determined by the free choices of consumers, businessmen and workers without the inflation.

But *if* the inflation were generally anticipated, and *if* society's economic arrangements should provide opportunities for everyone to adjust his economic contracts to take expected inflation into account, then the advantage of a stable price level over moderately rising prices in facilitating effective allocation of resources to meet consumer preferences would be largely eliminated. In principle, it is having an accurate basis on which to rest monetary expectations that is crucial, not the behavior of the price level *per se*. But if the "ifs" above are not fully met, and they certainly are not in the present American society, then the comparative advantage of price level stability may be substantial.

A counter-advantage of continuing inflation may lie in the lubrication it provides for a continually shifting pattern of resource use in a free choice, growing economy. When consumer demand shifts from buggies to autos, it is probably easier for workers to shift to automaking in response to the offer of higher wages there than to be forced out of buggy-making by declining wages and prices there. Thus in a gradually inflating economy, workers are nudged gently into new areas of consumer preference. Stable average prices mean a sharp pressure on declining industries and areas when demand shifts away, for their prices and incomes often must fall. Perhaps this painful, direct pressure to move is more effective than the positive pull of rising prices where demand increases. Observers differ. American agriculture over the past century has provided Exhibit A, from which resources have continually had to be transferred in large quantities. On the whole, excess workers have shifted to industry and the cities best in rising price periods. But the main lesson of history is that the shifts are relatively easy in booming, full employment periods, as contrasted to depression years. The advantage added by rising as against stable average prices is much less obvious.

How is the allocation of resources to meet consumer preferences best accomplished—by a stable or rising price level? Conclusion: a slight nod to price level stability, but many economists would vote, perhaps grudgingly, for slow inflation to ease the widespread shifts of resources required in a dynamic private choice economy.

(4) Would price level stability be more "equitable" than alternative price level policies?

What is "equity"? One common definition centers around the distribution of income: equity consists in greater equality in the distribution of income than is produced by the market system. On this test, there is little evidence from recent American experience that inflation produces major changes in the pattern of income distribution by size before taxes, one way or the other. Presumably the more effectively inflation is anticipated, the less will any such redistributional effect be—unless we assume, perhaps properly, that the wealthy are better at anticipating and adjusting to continuing inflation.

But this test is itself obviously unsatisfactory. There may be wide disagreements as to how much income should be redistributed, if at all. And some may say the "equitable" redistribution would be from young to old or vice versa, from workers to farmers or vice versa, from stockholders to union members or vice versa, or in any one of hundreds of other patterns. This way lies little hope in reaching an operationally clear, agreed definition of "equity."

*I suggest, instead, that for purposes of stabilization policy, "equity" consists in the non-disappointment of reasonable expectations*—essentially Jeremy Bentham's dictum of more than a century ago. This implies that the contribution of the government lies *not* in deciding exactly what income distribution should be forced on the public through inflation or other such devious routes. *Instead,* it lies in providing a predictable monetary basis for the formation of reasonable expectations, plus being sure that related governmental policies will not defeat such expectations or make it impossible for citizens to adjust their economic arrangements satisfactorily to their monetary expectations.

This is a philosophy that relies heavily on the individual to make the best choice as to what is good for himself, once the government provides a reasonable basis for forming expectations on those matters which it, rather than the individual, must control—in this case, the value of money. This position does not deny that a more or a less equal distribution of income may be better than the present one, *but merely that* such redistribution is the test of equity in monetary-fiscal policy. If we want to redistribute income from one group to another let us do so openly, not through the pretense of stabilization policies whose redistributional results are, at best, doubtful and devious.

If this definition of "equity" is accepted, it is clear that the choice between stable prices and inflation hinges on which provides a better basis for the formation of monetary expectations on which the economic system must operate. Price level stability obviously provides a straightforward, simple basis for such expectations. But an announced steady rate of inflation could, *in principle,* provide an equally satisfactory basis, *if* the rate were generally anticipated and *if* all income groups were able to adjust all their economic contracts accordingly. But these "ifs" are not met today. And short of an *announced* governmental policy of a stated rate of inflation plus widespread institutional changes to permit ready adjustment to rising average prices, it seems clear that price level stability is more "equitable" than any policy of rising (or falling) average prices.

(5) Lastly, would price level stability help more than moderate inflation to produce a workably viable socio-politico-economic society? I have argued above that peacetime inflation in America will be, in essence, a social-political process, of which monetary changes are more a manifestation than a cause. If this analysis is correct, this last question is a summary of all the others. Would continuing inflation be an effective social lubricant? Would it help conciliate the potentially explosive, persistent struggle for bigger income shares among the major economic groups in our society? Or would it be, instead, the disrupter of monetary and social stability that it has been so often painted in the major European inflations?

Lenin is said to have declared that the best way to destroy the Capitalist was to debauch the currency. J. M. Keynes has agreed:

"Lenin was certainly right. There is no subtler, no surer means of overturning the existing basis of society than to debauch the

63

currency. The process engages all the hidden forces of economic law on the side of destruction, and does it in a manner which not one man in a million is able to diagnose."[2]

More recently, Professor Martin Bronfenbrenner has suggested in a penetrating analysis not only that secular inflation is likely but also that it may provide an escape valve for the excess claims of competing income groups that will keep this income conflict from directly destroying the capitalist, free enterprise system.[3] According to Bronfenbrenner's analysis, the intensity of working class resentment against what they see to be excessive returns to property owners and business men has been steadily rising. For the individual worker, this feeling is not necessarily linked to any philosophical position that the share of wages in the national income should be increased. He merely wants higher wages when he sees the large profits reported by his company and others like it. But the result is the same either way. He pushes for a bigger wage share of the consumer's dollar. And there are lots of him, effectively organized.

What happens if this wage push eats heavily into profits? How big a shift in the present income shares from profits and interest (property income) to wages and salaries is consistent with the continued healthy operation of the present-type capitalist economy? Bronfenbrenner suggests that another 20 to 40 percent of the property income share might be shifted

[2] *The Economic Consequences of the Peace* (Harcourt Brace, 1920), p. 236.

[3] "Some Neglected Implications of Secular Inflation," in *Post-Keynesian Economics,* edited by K. K. Kurihari (Rutgers University Press, 1954). In the same volume, William Vickery presents a theoretical argument that long run economic stability is consistent with continuing inflation, and that inflation would have important advantages over stable prices: "Stability Through Inflation."

over to wages and salaries without undermining the mainspring of modern capitalism—the incentives to manage and to invest. This will be true especially if governmental monetary policy maintains interest rates at low levels so that more modest returns on investment will still provide appreciable margins over the cost of money. And he suggests that this much of an income transfer may well satisfy the claims of the working class for a good many years to come.

Whether Professor Bronfenbrenner's rough estimates are right or not, the crucial question here is whether gradual inflation would mollify significantly the income struggle. Would it extend the time period during which the politically powerful working class is satisfied with its income share, thereby postponing the day when a real crisis is faced for maintenance of investment incentives in the American capitalist system? Perhaps the effective rate of return on investment is already so low that new private investment cannot be counted on to maintain healthy economic growth; some "conservatives" argue this is the case. Perhaps the rate could drop much further than Bronfenbrenner suggests; some "liberals" and labor leaders argue that the danger point is far removed. But whether the danger point is near or far, to pretend that we will never reach it is merely to avoid facing what may soon or late become a very real problem indeed for the capitalist society we know.

Would continued or sporadic inflation mollify the income conflict that seems evident for the years ahead? Would it mislead either workers or investors enough to make them satisfied with higher money incomes even though their real incomes rose less rapidly? Would it content everyone even though his relative share of the total national output remained substantially constant? There is some evidence from the past that it may, to a limited extent, play this role of pacifier. The veil of money has not yet been drawn aside from many of the realities of economic life. It is on the answers to these questions that much of our policy toward inflation, I shall argue, must ultimately turn. Much of Chapter 4 is devoted to a more thorough look at the problems at stake here.

## III

To return to the question at the beginning of this chapter: how important an economic goal should maintenance of price level stability be for America today? I provisionally advance this proposition. Avoidance of inflation is a relevant and important social goal. But the real costs of moderate inflation are less than is widely supposed, especially *if* governmental policy provides a reasonable basis for monetary expectations, *if* prevailing economic arrangements permit people and organizations to adjust equally to expected inflation, *and if* we can be sure that moderate inflation does not swell to immoderate proportions. Clearly, the costs of inflation are different depending on the prevailing economic environment, the governmental policies in force, and the institutional arrangements under which economic groups can protect themselves against the fall in the value of money. Can we obtain the alleged benefits of "a litttle" inflation without undue hardship on those we wish to protect and without increasing the risk of galloping inflation? Or should we set our faces firmly against any inflation at all, facing the possible consequence of enforced unemployment if money wages rise rapidly? This is the question to which the next, and concluding, chapter is devoted.

# IV The Age of Inflation: Economics, Ethics, and Politics

WE LIVE IN AN AGE OF INFLATION, I have argued—not an age of rapid, continuous inflation, but one of intermittent, interrupted, yet persistent stair-step secular inflation. Prices rise when costs are bid up, when war spending swells, when total demand temporarily exceeds supply. Prices rise for many reasons; they will seldom fall far or for long. Underlying the entire process, the income claims of major economic groups exceed the total national real income available at current prices, as each group puts up its asking prices in order to increase its real income. Faced with this excess of claims, the government, committed to maintaining high level employment, will generally provide the additional purchasing power to support employment at the higher cost and price levels—indirectly through providing new money through the banks, or directly through fiscal policy.

Logically, once this process is well understood and government underwriting of high level employment is widely trusted, there is no end to the rate of inflation which may develop. But as a practical matter, the inflation is more likely to be a creeping one, outside of war periods—because economic groups and individuals are not yet confident enough of government policy to put aside caution, and because public fear of inflation is strong enough to restrain private and public action that conspicuously produces rapid price increases. Temporary periods of price stability are achieved when rises in money incomes seem sufficiently large, all things considered, temporarily to satisfy the major income groups. This temporary satisfaction may arise from conscious weighing of the costs of further upward pressure, or, more likely, when the money illusion has deceived income recipients into thinking their real incomes have risen more than they actually have.

One possible course of public policy is to permit this unplanned, unannounced secular inflation to occur. The economic consequences of such a mild inflationary drift, I argued above, are less drastic than many observers have claimed. Indeed, there are some possible economic gains from the process. Most important, skillful use of the money illusion might help to compromise excessive income claims without either rapid inflation or substantial unemployment, though this seems ever less likely as major groups adjust their claims effectively to rising prices.

But such an unannounced secular inflation must be rejected on grounds of equity, for the reasons argued in Chapter 3, even though its strictly economic consquences be tolerable. This is especially true since the inflation can occur only with the tacit or explicit consent of the government, which ultimately must provide, directly or indirectly, the additional money or direct purchasing power to support the ever-higher prices. And the chances of holding a government-supported inflation to only a few percent per year would surely weaken steadily as understanding of the process spread.

If, then, we rule out as desirable social policy an unplanned and unannounced inflationary drift which would gradually rob the ignorant and the generally passive income receivers of the economy for the benefit of the shrewd and the active, there seem to me to remain two major defensible alternatives. *The first* is to take a firm stand against inflation, facing realistically up to the problems this poses for maintaining full employment and to the political-economic problems of implementing the decision. *The second* is openly to accept the likelihood of secular inflation and to build into our economic life a thorough system of safeguards designed to protect participants in the economic process against the undersirable effects of inflation.

I propose in this concluding chapter to examine each of these two approaches, and then to suggest what seems to me the most acceptable set of policies for an age of inflation, balancing together the considerations of equity, economics, and politics.

## I

One morally defensible alternative is to check the inflation. This is clearly the intellectually most satisfying alternative— *if* we can do it, *and if* we can manage it without seriously impairing our chances of maintaining high level aggregate employment.

Mcrely to decide that the government "ought" to stabilize the price level solves no problems. Inflation in the modern society is a deep social and political phenomenon, if my analysis is correct. To be realistic, a policy of price level stabilization must face up to this fact.

To prevent a secular inflation, we need a stabilizer for the income struggle—a basis for a "truce" among the major contesting income groups. No one can blame labor for upholding its own interests in pushing for higher wages, especially in the face of rising prices where stable money wages mean falling real incomes. No one can blame businessmen for pushing up prices for higher profits under the same conditions. Yet it must be apparent that wage increases faster than the increase in productivity must mean either higher prices or decreasing real profits.

Price level stabilization—stable money—could provide an obviously fair and simple basis for such a truce, the keystone of a monetary framework within which the various income groups would have to settle their struggle for increased income shares primarily through the market, rather than in the halls of Washington with resulting persistent inflation. If both labor and management *knew* that monetary-fiscal policy would hold the price level stable, we can be sure that wage increases would come more slowly than now. With price level stabilization, the result of over-zealous wage or price increases would be unemployment or falling sales volume. Average money incomes in the economy could rise as fast as total output increased. Any faster increase would mean temporary unemployment of the out-of-line resources, since governmental policy would not provide the additional total demand required to bail out unemployment and falling sales.

The case for such a stable money policy is clear. It would provide an honest, simple basis for monetary expectations. It would set the "rules" for the income-share "game." Under a stable price level, the facts must be faced directly—total real incomes can rise only as fast as total real production increases. A faster increase for any income share necessarily means a slower one for some other. This straightforward policy would thrust the income contest back into the market place, or into open political debate when special economic groups seek political aid for larger incomes than the market justifies, as in the case of farm parity prices.

It woud be foolish to underestimate the likelihood that a strong stable money policy would involve some unemployment, possibly a substantial amount. Recognition that excessively rapid wage and price increases must mean loss of sales and of jobs will not come easily, however readily union and business leaders may agree in principle that inflation must be avoided.

Suppose a price stabilization policy has been firmly announced by the government and suppose further that both labor and management are convinced that the government will live up to its policy. Company A knows full well that if it and other companies agree to a big wage increase they must either take a profit squeeze or risk losing sales through a price increase, if total purchasing power is held down by monetary policy. The union knows the same facts, though it probably has a different view as to how far profits could reasonably be squeezed. What would you do if you were the union leader?

Maybe you'd scale down your asking wage to a figure that would be obviously reasonable to management. But the chances are you wouldn't—at least not at first. You'd like to get as much as possible for your members, and profits probably look fatter to you than they need to be. More important, especially if you're head of a small union, you won't see why a little higher wage for your men will be important enough to make any difference on the national scene. Even if your employer has to put up his price a little he can surely keep up his sales with a little extra effort.

Now what if you're the company president across the bargaining table. Will you give in on a wage that requires a price increase? Not if you can help it, and you will fight bitterly if the increase would push your prices above your competitors. But what if the union pushes hard and the alternative is to take a strike? Suppose you're a big glass company making windshields for Pontiac. Will you take the strike and risk closing down Pontiac, which runs on a low inventory of windshields? Maybe, but if you do you'd better be ready to start looking for some other business to replace that lucrative Pontiac order, because Pontiac isn't going to be very happy if it has to shut down and lose sales to Mercury and Dodge. So there's a good chance you'll bargain as hard as you can, but ultimately settle to keep production going, even if the wage is higher than you can stand without boosting your prices.[1]

Where is monetary policy to take hold in this setting? The Federal Reserve Board can ultimately limit the size of the money supply and check inflation. But it is far away and only dimly understood. Yet if many unions and firms behave like you and prices begin to creep up, the Federal Reserve's task is clear—hold down the money supply to shut off the funds necessary to finance the higher prices. Actually, all the Federal Reserve needs to do is sit tight, just seeing to it that total bank credit stays at about its present figure. Though there's always some leeway, before long the shortage of money will check the rising prices—through the fact that sales will fall off as prices rise. And falling sales mean unemployment.

Indeed, recently it has become stylish to speak of the cost-push administered-price phenomenon as a "new type of inflation," quite different in cause than a "demand-pull" inflation and quite unsusceptible to control through the traditional means

[1] Leland Hazard, a senior corporation executive, has painted a realistic picture of management motives and behavior in wage bargaining under such circumstances. See: "What Economists Don't Know About Wages," *Harvard Business Review*, January-February, 1957.

of limiting total monetary demand. Even with a stable money supply, increased spending may be financed by a faster rate of money turnover. In early 1957, for example, prices continued to rise moderately in spite of higher interest rates and obviously tight money for many borrowers. This, some observers argued, demonstrated that monetary restriction is of no avail against "the new inflation."

But surely this is a myopic view. It is clear that monetary-fiscal policy has a harder job in an economy of administered prices. Its impact is slower, and less predictable in any short period. The credit squeeze falls unequally on different firms and different industries; in general, the least credit-worthy— often the smaller, highly competitive firms—feel the pinch of monetary restriction first. But slower though the check may be, shortage of total monetary demand is one sure way of checking the inflation. No firm, however administered its prices and however protected its market, will long continue to raise its prices if its sales decline substantially. And the rate of turnover of money cannot increase greatly without either widespread institutional changes or real inflation panic. History shows no long-continued, major inflation yet without a major increase in the money supply. There is no reason to suppose today is different on this score. Tight money may be slow and imprecise. But it is powerful indeed if we stick to it.

There is some hope that restrictive monetary policy can get directly at oligopolistic, administered-price firms. To push up prices as costs rise in the face of weak demand, the firm must pile up inventory or cut back output. The latter is painful indeed; its implies lower sales volume and probably loss of market position. But if the firm temporarily accumulates inventory while waiting for the hoped-for increase in consumer demand, it must have added funds to carry this inventory and meet other interim costs. Here is a channel, though only a partial one, whereby tight money can strike directly at the price increases of those administered-price firms which seem most insulated from monetary policy.

But ultimately the bite of a stable money policy must probably come on sales and employment, at least until both workers and businessmen become fully impressed that the government means what it says about refusing to support inflation. Even thereafter, can we hope that the painful lesson of unemployment would restrain most of the individual bargainers who make up the American economy and who set the individual wages and prices that together comprise the wage and price levels of the economy?

To expect the big unions and the big industries eventually to learn the lesson if the government really follows such a policy is surely reasonable, unhappy though they may be. And big business and big labor are the leaders, the pattern-setters. But even if they do learn, would the myriads of smaller units stay in line? And would even the individual pattern-setters long be able to follow "reasonable" policies, without the repeated reminder of unemployment?

Some observers look toward increasing responsibility from both unions and management through increased bargaining areas. Where one union fears to moderate its wage demands lest others obtain larger benefits for their members, grouping many unions together might move toward a national wage policy, more responsible and more cognizant of the national consequences of wage demands. Similarly, industry-wide groups of employers might have to give more weight to the national consequences of price increases resulting from inflationary bargains, than do the individual companies which largely comprise today's bargaining units. Examples along this path are England and Sweden, where the unions act jointly for many purposes and where they share major political responsibility in the national legislatures. Some say that these arrangements have worked well. Labor, in spite of its powerful position, has held its wage demands well below what it politically might have exacted, at least in Sweden. But these demands have not been low enough to avoid persistent inflation. And the skeptic may argue that only the pressure of the export market, where Swedish and British goods must compete for direly needed foreign exchange, has held the unions thus far in check. Certainly inflation, not unemployment, has followed persistent wage increases, as monetary policy has reluctantly acceded to the necessity for more purchasing power. The experience has been neither happy nor without hope.

Believers in individual monetary incentive will prefer another tack. What we need is measures to provide stronger incentives for businessmen to resist wage demands, and for unions to moderate their demands. Exhortation makes for fine news stories, but seldom influences men against their own self-interest, the argument runs. Union leaders and business statesmen will expound the need for moderation to avoid inflation, but in the end they will generally settle for higher wages and higher prices if they are convinced that is best for their own private interests.

No one has come up yet with very convincing steps to provide this individual incentive toward general moderation in an age of inflation. Removal of the corporation income tax so the government would not bear half the cost of wage increases has been suggested, with replacement of the lost funds through a non-income tax on businesses. Perhaps this would increase the incentive to resist. Greater security for union leaders, to permit them to exercise greater statesmanship in wage demands without fear of being overthrown by employers or rival leaders might help. Enforcement of more vigorous competition among businesses would increase the reluctance of any individual firm to grant price-raising cost increases. This is, in principle, the most promising suggestion—increase the danger of market loss faced by any manager who gives in to inflationary wage demands. But as a practical matter, the problems are great. The individual employer can be whipsawed by the big union, and he will think a long time before he takes a strike that alienates his major customers. Remember the Pontiac order. Other suggestions have been made—but not many. No easy answer appears.

Firm governmental action to prevent inflation would face grave political and economic problems. It may be politically and economically unrealistic, even though it is ethically attractive. But there is little doubt that the masses fear and distrust inflation, and that stable money has a real rallying ring. And what we need most is a real "religion" of money to introduce a stabilizer into the inflationary politico-economic income and power struggle. The claim for price stabilization is not that it is, in principle, much better than any other clearly announced, simple monetary policy (such as prices rising steadily at say 2 percent per annum). The basic case is, instead, that stable money may provide a better rallying cry for popular support for a firm monetary policy in time of stress. For stress there will be when unions push up wages faster than productivity. For either management must resist with resulting strikes, or it must raise prices to reflect higher wage costs with resulting loss of sales and unemployment until wages and prices are forced back into line with what the market will bear.[2]

In a democracy where major power groups clash, no policy can long stand which does not command a substantial consensus from the citizenry. Ultimately there can be no continuing rule or authority beyond the strength that it commands through popular support. As a temporary expedient, "outbargaining" the various groups of the public may work satisfactorily for the monetary authority; but without a "religion" of money on which to anchor (perhaps unreasoning) public confidence and support, the policy is self-doomed. As Henry C. Simons has eloquently put the core of the issue:

The modern test of truth (in public policy formation) is simply voluntary rational consensus. . . . The good, progressive moral order must rest on intelligent consensus and on much the same kind of free, critical discussion as is involved in scientific inquiry. The social processes of a free society are, if not infallible, the only reliable means to moral truth and the best means to security under law.[3]

In the end, Simons is surely right. If we want to preserve the value of our monetary unit, the compromise of conflicting income interests can ultimately be solved only on the grounds of a working voluntary consensus—not by hoping to fool most of the people most of the time. A workable plan for price stability in a democracy must be one in which income claims *are* sufficiently stabilized to permit full employment without

[2] For more complete analyses of the possibilities and problems of price level stabilization, see G. L. Bach, "Rearmament, Recovery and Monetary Policy," *American Economic Review* (March, 1941) pp. 27-41; and "Monetary-Fiscal Policy Reconsidered," *Journal of Political Economy,* October, 1949, and reprinted in *Readings in Fiscal Policy,* A. Smithies and J. K. Butters, editors (Irwin, 1955).

[3] *Economic Policy for a Free Society* (University of Chicago Press, 1947), pp. 8-9.

inflation, under the restraint of voluntary consensus of support for the stabilization plan.

## II

The other morally defensible alternative is, accepting the likelihood of secular inflation, to build into our economic arrangements a system of safeguards designed to minimize the inequities of persistently rising prices. Americans are not used to the notion of secular inflation. We, as a people, have no thorough defenses against rising prices. Our mores and our economic institutions presume that the value of the monetary unit will be reasonably stable. If we accept rising prices, we must face up to a wholesale reevaluation of our economic practices. As the London *Economist* has suggested: We have made our inflationary bed and we must lie on it—but we might as well be reasonably comfortable.[4]

Inflation has been called "the silent robber." But we can largely neutralize its effects by seeing that everyone robs everyone else at about the same rate. This means seeing that all prices rise at about the same rate, or at least permitting people to make such arrangements if they want to. A thorough set of measures to assure this result would include the following:

(1) Wages and salaries should be tied to a cost-of-living index. This would immediately immunize something like two-thirds of the entire income structure against loss from inflation on current income account. By guaranteeing this type of protection, this change should help also to prevent strikes which otherwise might arise from controversies over the amount of wage increases needed to protect workers against unknown

[4] "Agenda for the Age of Inflation—II," *The Economist,* August 25, 1951, provides a lively blueprint for an inflation-proof economy, along even more drastic lines than those outlined here. My indebtedness will be obvious.

amounts of inflation during the life of the contract. The change, incidentally, would not be costless. Inflation has long been a valuable wartime device to transfer purchasing power from workers to finance war production as wages lagged behind government-induced rising prices. With wages tied to prices, inflation would lose this possible war-period usefulness as a tool of war finance—if, indeed, we have not already lost it without formal escalation.

(2) Business accounting conventions should be drastically changed, to recognize that a dollar is *not* a dollar in the constant-purchasing-power sense our prevailing accounting theory presumes. While there may be reasons to continue the present tradition of carrying assets on business balance sheets at their historical costs, it is clear that inflation makes these values substantially meaningless for many current operating and investment problems.

In a world of inflation, we must begin to reckon depreciation charges in terms that will replace the depreciating assets at current prices, not at their misleading historical costs. Similarly, cost of goods sold should be calculated on the basis of current replacement cost of materials used, rather than on their historical cost. Without these changes reported business profits will always be larger than "real" profits, and the difference may easily be so big as to be drastically misleading from business management, investment, and public policy viewpoints.

An example is provided by a recent study sponsored by the American Accounting Association of the effect of inflation on a sample of four companies from 1940 to 1952, referred to above.[5] In all four, reported profits were far in excess of "real"

[5] Ralph C. Jones, *Price Level Changes and Financial Statements: Case Studies of Four Companies.* See also George Terborgh, *Corporate Profits in the Decade 1947-1956,* cited above.

profits (that is, profits after adjustment was made for price increases). On the average, "real" profits were just about half those reported. Although all four companies showed apparent large financial gains for their stockholders over the period, actually the real value of stockholders' equity in the companies rose only slightly over the prosperous decade, and actually declined in one case.

There can be little excuse for pretending that business profits are far larger than they actually are by permitting inflation to obscure the facts. This confuses management, investors, labor, and the general public, who can find out what is really going on only through a major analytical study to separate out the real progress of the company in an age of inflation. To reckon all depreciation charges and costs of inventory sold on a current replacement cost basis would remedy much of the deception, and less can hardly be justified under a policy of accepted inflation. "Lifo" (last in, first out) inventory accounting, which is now widely used after two decades of inflation, goes some distance in this direction, but by no means the whole way. There are some difficult accounting problems involved in using constant-purchasing-power accounting—some of which are noted later on—but this should not obscure the central need for reform. Ideally, companies should maintain records showing profits calculated on the present "old-style" basis *and* on a constant-purchasing-power basis, so investors and management could separate the effects of operations and of inflation in assessing results and making plans.

(3) Paralleling this change in accounting practice, the government should change its taxing policies to permit costs to be charged as indicated above. Since the corporation income tax falls on reported profit, not on real profit adjusted for in-

flation, the actual tax rate is higher than the apparent rate. In the study indicated just above, the actual rate ranged from about 25 to 50 percent higher than the apparent rate, when the "real" profit base was used rather than the reported, inflated figures. Thus, because of this enforced underreporting of costs, corporations pay a much higher effective tax rate in inflationary times than is commonly supposed. We may decide to tax profits as heavily as we like, but we should surely tax them honestly and openly, net of replacement costs for plant, equipment and materials used up in production.

(4) More generally, the government should shift its own financial practices to treat fairly those with whom it deals. Where it is a dominant employer, as in hiring government workers and teachers, it should tie its own wages to a cost-of-living index. Where it regulates private business, it should abandon its traditional practice of lagging behind rising prices elsewhere in the economy—not only for reasons of equity, but because failure to do so means an uneconomical shift of resources out of the government-controlled area. Notable examples in the American inflation are the persistent, drastic shortage of highly skilled government workers and of teachers, the undermaintained condition of the nation's railroads, and the persistent post-war shortage of telephone equipment. It is dubious policy indeed for the government to "set a good example," when in fact the example merely robs the public it pretends to induce to better behavior.

(5) In borrowing money, the government should issue its securities, or at least part of them, on a constant-purchasing-power basis. That is, its bonds should be repayable in a variable number of dollars but in a constant amount of purchasing power. If the price level doubles during the life of the bond, the bondholder would get back twice the number of dollars he

originally loaned to the government. Probably interest on securities should be similarly denominated in constant-purchasing-power units, though here the advantages less clearly outweigh the complications. This shift, it should be noted, could help the government as well as the investor, since in an age of inflation the interest rate on such bonds would be substantially lower than on the traditional variety. But most important, there can be little excuse for the government itself seizing capital from the weak and the ignorant from whom it borrows on the pretext that government bonds are "the safest investment you can make."

(6) Present regulations requiring trust funds and fiduciaries of all sorts to invest primarily in fixed interest obligations should be abolished. Indeed, there would be a reasonable case for substituting the precisely opposite requirement, that trustees be *prohibited* from investing at all in such fixed interest securities.[6] Where the trust agreement is between competent, well informed parties, private parties can safely be left to decide for themselves the type of contract they prefer. But in a vast range of retirement plans and other trust agreements, the individual has either little control over the arrangements or inadequate knowledge to look out effectively for his own interests. Here drastic revision of the present legal restrictions to fixed-income investments would be essential.

At the end of 1956, for example, apparently over $25 billion was already accumulated in private company retirement plans for employees, largely compulsory and largely managed by or through the companies concerned. This total is growing now at probably $3 billion a year, and the rate of

[6] Strikingly, German trustees were released from the legal requirement to invest only in approved, fixed-income type assets and real estate only in 1923, by which time the real value of the trust funds invested in bonds and money had vanished.

increase is rising steadily. Governmental social security, which draws nearly $10 billion annually of compulsory contributions and affects nearly 100 million people, should of course be the leader in transferring to a cost-of-living adjustment basis. A similar principle applies for government benefits to widows, children, the blind, and other such groups.

(7) More generally, all private contracts should be clearly enforceable on a constant-purchasing-power basis, and present legal restraints against such contracts should be removed. While private borrowers and lenders can safely be left to decide for themselves the basis on which they wish to denominate their contracts (with the interest rate presumably much lower on constant-purchasing-power debts), there can be little case for prohibiting savers from access to constant purchasing power assets, or borrowers from issuing such securities if they wish to do so. The law at present in many countries casts doubt on the enforceability of such contracts, and regulatory practice drastically limits the issue of such securities. Moreover, insurance companies are specifically forbidden to sell insurance or annuities denominated in variable dollar amounts.[7] All such restrictions should be removed.

If we should adopt these measures, or even most of them, the inequities of moderate inflation would be largely eliminated. Though secular inflation would still rob the holders of money of part of its value and though even these measures could not hope to protect each individual from all the impact of inflation, the program would see that most of the fraud of inflation was offset by giving everyone more money to buy at higher prices.

[7] See F. A. Mann, *The Legal Aspect of Money* (London, 1953) Ch. 4, for the legal status of such contracts in various countries.

It may be objected that this set of measures would increase the likelihood of inflation, by removing everyone's fear that inflation would rob him. This is true. The price we would pay for a reasonable protection against the inequities of inflation is even greater inflation.

## III

How shall we choose between these paths of action—*the one* to fight inflation and risk the cost of unemployment, *the other* to accept inflation but build in a thorough-going set of safeguards that will negate many of its effects? Which alternative is most attractive ethically, sound economically and feasible politically?

The conclusion must be, I think, that we should take a major stand against inflation, however hard this path may be. Not that moderate inflation is a major disaster. The redistributional inequities of moderate inflation are less than is often claimed, and they could be further lessened by adoption of the measures outlined in the preceding section. But the gains from continually rising prices as a social lubricant and mollifier of class conflict are largely illusory, and the costs of the galloping inflation we risk if we wipe out general faith in stable money are too great to hazard. Inflation results when total monetary claims on goods and services rise faster than goods and services available. It resolves this conflict of excessive income claims only by pushing up prices until enough people are cheated out of their expectations to make total demand and supply balance again. If we remove most of the danger that inflation will rob anyone but continue the social and economic machinery that generates and supports inflation, where the process ends short of galloping inflation is hard to see. Inflation will become unable to cheat people of their expectations, since people will lose their presumption of stable monetary values and increasingly anticipate further price rises in their income claims.

The major safeguard against runaway inflation is precisely the fear that inflation brings dire consequences for millions of people, coupled with a long-standing belief that there is something inherently good and sound about stable money. We must maintain a widespread faith in money if we expect people to continue to hold and use money in a reasonable fashion. Once this faith seriously weakens, the potential price is enormous—in inequities too great for even built-in safeguards to prevent, and in real disruption and economic waste far beyond those seen in moderate inflation.

We should choose the course of honesty rather than monetary illusion. But, at least for the foreseeable future, some inflationary drift is probably inescapable, however hard we try to avoid it. General acceptance of stable money as a framework for income bargaining is, from a social viewpoint, clearly beneficial. But there is no blinking at the fact that some sellers may try to increase their shares of the income pie by claiming more than they can get without a serious invasion of others' shares. And when many important sellers behave this way, to impose the penalty of temporary unemployment rather than permitting inflation to ease the crisis is a Spartan government policy that can stand only with widespread support and understanding.

If some inflation is likely to occur in spite of our best efforts to avoid it, equity surely requires that the government (which must ultimately condone inflation for it to occur) in the meantime offer reasonable safeguards against the redistributional inequities of rising prices, even though those safeguards decrease the chance of completely avoiding inflation itself. Two classes of action, suggested above, could remove much of the inequity without substantially undercutting the struggle against inflation.

First, the government itself should have clean hands. In its own dealings it should not *require* citizens to behave as if the dollar were stable in value. Second, the government should permit individuals and businesses to make private contracts to protect themselves against inflation, as long as these contracts do no harm to others. Consider each briefly.

(1) The government should have clean hands in its own dealings. Specifically:

(a) Business income tax law should be amended to *permit* calculation of taxable profits on a basis using price-level-adjusted inventory and depreciation costs, or possibly price-level-adjusted total profits. Part of this alternative is now available to businesses through the use of "Lifo" inventory accounting. At a minimum, a comparable alternative should be available on the computation of depreciation charges entered as costs of production. The businessman who chooses such partial or completely price-level-adjusted tax accounting would, of course, assume the risk of higher taxes than under present methods if the price level should fall rather than rise.[8]

This fact that business taxes are partly levied on fictitious profits does *not* necessarily mean, as many businessmen have claimed, that business income taxes are

[8] There is a large literature on the advantages, disadvantages, and problems involved in such price-level-adjusted accounting. See especially R. C. Jones, *Effects of Price Level Changes on Business Income, Capital, and Taxes,* cited above; and "Price Level Changes and Financial Statements: Supplementary Statement No. 2 by the Committee on Concepts and Standards Underlying Corporate Financial Statements of the American Accounting Association," *The Accounting Review,* October, 1951.

too high. The contribution businesses should make to the total governmental tax take is properly decided by Congress, reflecting the popular will, just as in the case of other taxes. What the present situation does mean is, first, that we do not really know what the business tax burden is in relation to real (price-adjusted) profits; and second, that substantial inequities are created between firms for whom depreciation and inventory costs play substantially different roles. With secular inflation, the actual corporation income tax rate is higher than the apparent rate. There can be little excuse for kidding ourselves that corporations are paying lower rates on their actual profits than is the case, or for treating different types of businesses differently taxwise merely because accounting tradition copes inadequately with the age of inflation. A more defensible alternative would be to compute taxes on actual (price-adjusted) profits wherever corporations choose this accounting convention, and then to raise corporation tax rates to whatever new level is required if we want the total corporate tax burden to remain at its present dollar level.

(b) In issuing its own securities the government should include at least one stable purchasing power bond—that is, a bond on which principal (and possibly interest) is payable in a stable amount of purchasing power rather than a fixed number of dollars. Such a bond could readily be based on a simple cost-of-living adjustment through the regular Bureau of Labor Statistics consumer price index. Such a security would presumably be salable at a substantially lower rate of interest than are regular bonds of comparable duration if the likelihood of inflation is serious.

It is sometimes objected (for example by the Treasury itself) that such a bond is unacceptable because it involves a potential unlimited liability of the Treasury, in case prices should rise in the future. But this is exactly the liability the Treasury should have. Any other position is to say that the government itself may wish to defraud its citizens through borrowing good dollars and repaying bad. If, with the alternative of constant-purchasing-power securities available, investors choose to buy traditional bonds, the government can hardly be criticized. The function of the government is not to make decisions for its citizens but rather to provide honest information and reasonable alternatives on which individuals can make their own judgments. If, in fact, the value of money (which is surely the government's responsibility) remains stable, the happy result will be that the Treasury has borrowed at a lower interest cost through the issue of constant-purchasing-power bonds, while citizens have been able to avail themselves of protection against loss of savings through government-supported inflation. This action would not be novel. Both the Finnish and French governments, for example, have issues of this sort.[9]

[9] Brief analyses of constant-purchasing-power bonds for the United States are provided by G. L. Bach and R. A. Musgrave, "A Stable Purchasing Power Bond," *American Economic Review,* December, 1941; and Richard Goode, "A Constant Purchasing-Power Bond," *National Tax Journal,* December, 1951. A broader study, covering public and private experiences in several nations, is David Finch, "Purchasing Power Guarantees for Deferred Payments," *International Monetary Fund Staff Papers,* February, 1956. France, attempting to encourage savings and to finance government spending without corresponding taxes, has experimented with some of the most novel issues. One bond, in 1956, carried an interest payment that would rise automatically in proportion to the total French gross national (money)

(c) Governments should put all prices which they determine unilaterally on something like a cost-of-living-adjusted basis. This covers especially salaries of government employees and teachers, and the prices charged by public utilities under government regulation. To fail to do so is morally indefensible and generally economically inefficient. Formal government use of a price-level-adjustment formula is not essential, and probably not even desirable. But to use government-established prices as a "good example" in holding back inflation is a dubious practice.

(2) In addition to coming with clean hands itself, the government should avoid prohibiting individuals and businesses from making private contracts to protect themselves against possible inflation, as long as these contracts cause no harm to others. For example, in a world where persistent inflation seems likely, to forbid insurance companies and trustees of many classes to invest the great bulk of the funds they presumably protect in any except fixed-income securities is indeed a perversion of "protection." Similarly, refusal to permit insurance companies to sell "variable annuities," with proper safeguards of course, seems indefensible.

The duty of the government here is to provide a reasonable basis for the monetary expectations of its citizens, and probably to see that fiduciaries and financial intermediaries meet special standards of morality and probity. At a minimum,

---

product (*New York Times*, June 18, 1956). Another went even further, providing automatic inflation protection on both principal and interest payments, plus a nominal interest rate of 5 percent compared to the then-prevailing yield of 3 percent on high grade French stocks, plus a guarantee of the original face value repayment in francs in case of falling prices, plus eligibility of the bonds for use in paying taxes before maturity (*Time* Magazine, September 17, 1956).

savings institutions and trustees should surely be required to make clear to savers what they propose to do with the money placed with them. But for the government to require such financial middlemen to invest in inflation-vulnerable bonds and to forbid them the right to offer counter-inflation opportunities on a full-information basis to savers who wish them, verges on requiring some savers to suffer unprotected the inflation which the government directly or permissively imposes on them.

The controversy currently raging between our two largest insurance giants—the Metropolitan and the Prudential—over the issue of "variable annuities" poses the issue for current policy. Unfortunately, much of the argument appears to develop more heat than light. But the central issue is this: Should savers who wish to do so have a right to buy through highly reputable insurance companies retirement annuities stated not in a constant number of dollars but rather in a variable number of dollars that will shift very roughly with changes in the general price level? Savers' funds would be invested largely in common stocks, and annuity payments would depend on the course of stock prices and dividends. If my analysis of the outlook for inflation is correct, it is hard to see how the answer can be no, once adequate safeguards of full information on the new annuities are established. Yet no insurance company may sell such annuities to the American public today under regulations of the dominant state insurance agencies.

The Prudential says that inflation is a reality and that it may well continue in the future. The real value of savings invested in traditional insurance and annuities has been cruelly slashed by inflation, not once but repeatedly. Annuities based on the return on common stocks might indeed fluctuate in dollar

amount, but in a loose way and over the long run these fluc-
tuations will parallel major changes in the price level, thus
providing considerable protection for the annuitant against
*major* inflation in the future. If corporation dividends and stock
prices fall, as they certainly may from time to time, the variable annuity holder will receive fewer dollars. But such de-
clines will come primarily when prices generally are falling,
and over the longer pull the outlook for common stock prices
and dividends is clearly up as the economy grows, even in the
absence of inflation. The best alternative would be to prevent
inflation. But since that happy result is far from sure, we would
like to sell variable annuities to the public, not to replace but
to supplement the more traditional annuities for those who
prefer the common stock investment pattern, with fluctuating
dollar yields, to the fixed dollar variety. So says the Prudential.[10]

The Metropolitan disagrees sharply. Basically, it argues that
variable annuities would be devices for playing the stock
market, not annuities. It points out that stock prices have
dropped much further than the cost of living in many past
recessions, so the apparent protection against contingencies
for the annuitant would be illusory. More important, the Met-

---

[10] For an official statement of the case, see, for example, "The Need
for Variable Annuities," a statement by Carrol M. Shanks, President
of the Prudential Insurance Company of America, before the Business
Affairs Committee of the New Jersey State Legislature on May 13,
1955. The counterargument is presented by Frederic W. Ecker, President of the Metropolitan Life Insurance Company, in "Variable Annuities," an address before the Texas Life Convention on October 19,
1956. Copies of these and related statements are happily provided by
the respective companies. A general evaluation of variable annuities,
including a report on their experimental use by the Teachers Insurance
and Annuity Association for university teachers, is provided by Leon-
ard Morrisey, "The Dispute Over the Variable Annuity," *Harvard
Business Review,* January-February, 1957.

ropolitan argues that the public would like variable annuities fine as long as stock prices and dividends were rising, but in a downturn people would not only turn against the issuing companies but would also lose their faith in the whole institution of life insurance and the life insurance companies.

Variable annuities would indeed be riskier in terms of the number of dollars received than are present fixed-income annuities. And the Metropolitan may be right that some buyers would be only fair-weather friends of the insurance companies. But the issue is not whether variable annuities should replace the traditional variety. It is merely whether an insurance company will be *permitted* to offer such annuities for sale on a *voluntary* basis to buyers, supplementary to its more traditional offerings. Put in terms of private savers, the issue is whether those who wish to purchase a different type of insurance company annuity may do so—a policy riskier in terms of dollars but safer in the fundamental sense of purchasing power if in fact the outlook is for substantial inflation. Put in these terms, it is hard to see how the government can reasonably refuse private companies and citizens the right to contract privately to protect themselves against possible inflation, even though the arrangements deviate substantially from traditional insurance patterns.

It may be objected that even the modest governmental policies outlined in this section as supplements to a major stand against inflation would constitute open government pronouncement of the inevitability of inflation. This, I think, is not true. Each of the measures indicated is merely permissive, except for the more rapid catching-up of government-set prices to inflation if it occurs. In each case, citizens directly affected by government action or regulation are merely given an option to act to protect themselves against rising prices if they choose to do so, sometimes at an appreciable cost or risk to themselves in case prices should fall instead. To go less far in providing this option for those who rely directly on government behavior can hardly be tolerated ethically in a world where at least some inflation, reluctantly supported by government monetary policy, is probable. To go much farther risks speeding the inflation we seek to avoid.

Each of the policies advanced, except for business tax reform which stands firmly on its own merits, is aimed to protect the weak and the relatively uninformed, many of whom inescapably look to the government for protection. Most other groups hardly need more protection. Indeed, the lesson of the American inflation since 1939, if I read it correctly, is that the active major economic groups all managed to defend their income shares effectively. The wage-earners have managed to increase their share substantially at the expense of the passive groups—especially the aged, the retired, the savers, and those directly dependent on government. The danger is not that the major active groups will fall behind in inflation, but rather that their income claims will rise so rapidly, even without government aid, that preservation of the value of the dollar will be impossible.

## IV

I have said nothing of the use of direct governmental controls over individual wages and prices as a measure against inflation. This is partly because general acceptance of widespread government wage and price controls in peacetime seems to me out of the question. But more important, government direct wage-price controls against inflation would solve nothing in the world I have described. In the American democratic society, the peacetime inflation problem will be that the powerful, active groups are unwilling to enforce or accept discipline on their wage and price behavior so as to avoid inflation. If we should have a system of direct wage-price controls, holding the line would depend on the willingness of precisely these same powerful politico-economic groups to see themselves disciplined.

Perhaps a peacetime system of direct wage-price controls might provide a modest political rallying ground for the economically passive groups who largely stand to lose from inflation. Perhaps it would dramatize the wage and price increases by bringing them up for public hearing and justification. Perhaps, in short, it might provide some drag on the inflationary process. But ultimately its success would hinge on the same broad public support for, and insistence on, moderation of income claims that will be required for a stable price level without direct controls. And the public antipathy to direct government interference in wage and price setting, plus the extensive real costs of thoroughgoing government intervention in the entire price and wage structure which allocates our resources, combine to make this path not only unlikely but also unattractive to the economic liberal whose basic faith rests in individual choice and the market place.

V

This, then, is the basic dilemma faced in determining public policy in an age of inflation. On the one hand, the value of money can be protected only through common understanding of the necessity for compromise of income claims within a framework of monetary stability. In the end, only voluntary consensus on the advantage of price stability and the illusory nature of the gains from persistent inflation can provide a reasonable chance of both high level employment and stable prices. To obtain price level stability we must have public understanding of the dangers of "income claims," or "pressure group," inflation.

But on the other hand, this very understanding pulls aside the mysterious, cloudy veil of money and shows clearly the power of monetary-fiscal policy to provide purchasing power to bail out unemployment. By wiping out ignorance, we wipe out much of the fear that provides a major barrier against inflation. In a society with full understanding of "democratic" pressure group inflation, the logical conclusion is a political economy of power groups—each coldly calculating the rate of wage or price advance best designed to maximize its share of the national real income; each recognizing that government dare not let excessive demands generate widespread unemployment; and each fully aware that inflation, if it occurs, will transfer real income from the passive, fixed income groups and from savers generally to the active power groups.

This is a situation to strike terror to the heart of any experienced mediator—when all the extraneous facts and side-issues have been stripped away and powerful adversaries face each other on a crystal sharp issue where one or the other must give way in full view of everyone concerned. Somehow the democratic process must minimize these crises in compromising income claims, preferably by thrusting the bargain back into the accepted framework of the market place. The hope for the democratic society generally lies in the multiplicity of allegiances of the participants in the process—allegiances to family, to company, to union, to state, to church, and to many others. That the democratic process can work effectively seems precariously doubtful if economic allegiances become unified and few, in a clearcut focus on income shares with no diversionary danger or loss for the major contestants.

I see no real solution to this dilemma short of an agreed return of the income bargaining process to the framework of the market place bounded by stable money mores. And even this "solution" faces severe problems. In the end, we will have full employment without inflation only if the public wants this result, understands broadly the necessary conditions for its achievement, and is willing to pay the costs of restraint involved.

But other observers, especially many financial conservatives, suggest what seems to them an easy solution. Make the Federal Reserve strong and fully independent, they say. Staff it with far-seeing and dedicated men, and direct them to deny the inflation. This they will do by refusing to provide the funds to bail out inflationary demands—by unions, by business, by agriculture, or by the government itself. In support, they point especially to the events of the past few years where tight money has surely helped to restrain the inflationary process.

This, I suggest, is an appealing but illusory picture. The inflationary pressures I have described are deeply rooted in our economic and political institutions. To suppose that any small group of men, however prestigious their institution, can long impose its will on the American people to enforce stable prices even at the cost of widespread unemployment seems to me naive. The Federal Reserve System was established by Congress and the signature of a President. It can be changed overnight or abolished in the same way. The Federal Reserve's actions will be respected and tolerated as long as they are, basically, wanted by the public. Little longer!

A Federal Reserve Board substantially independent of the federal Treasury is indeed a partial check on irresponsible Treasury behavior in handling the federal debt. But a Federal Reserve Board fully independent of the President and the entire executive branch of the government, or even more of the Congress itself, could work only if there were no serious conflict between its policies and those of the government. For the government does reflect the views of the public, more closely and quickly than many of us are willing to admit, and the public will tolerate a check upon itself only so long as it basically wants the check to be exercised.

The history of Federal Reserve action since the monetary "accord" of 1951 shows, I believe, a central bank in substantial agreement with the desires of a majority of the public and of the President and Congress. While minor differences of interpretation of current economic winds have arisen from time to time, the cautious but firm position of the Reserve authorities against inflation has been what Mr. Eisenhower has wanted, and most members of Congress and the public as well. Thus, the past five years have not demonstrated the power of an independent Federal Reserve to check inflation against the wishes of the government and the "politicians." Rather, I suggest, it has demonstrated the usefulness of a social institution that can operate effectively as a part of the government, but sufficiently apart from the day-to-day pressures of operating government to be able to take a stronger stand against inflation than the administration and the Congress like to take openly, however much they basically agree with it.

This interpretation, if it is correct, argues not that we could expect a more independent Federal Reserve to serve as a stronger bulwark against inflation. Instead it argues that a Federal Reserve working cooperatively with a friendly administration can play a role that would be far more difficult for a governmental agency without a substantial show of independence. Perhaps the pretense of Federal Reserve independence could be usefully strengthened, though I doubt it. In the formation of the basic economic policy of the government, I suspect that the influence of the Federal Reserve toward monetary stability will be stronger if it is heard in the policy-making councils than if it must arbitrarily attempt to thwart the policies of the government from outside.[11]

But most important, we shall be misguided indeed if we pretend that a more "'independent" Federal Reserve, or any other group of wise men or experts, can guarantee us against inflation unless the American public accepts the necessity to hold its income claims down to the goods and services available at stable prices. It is striking that Federal Reserve policy has not been able to maintain price stability over the past year, even with weak farm prices and the strong moral support of both the President and most of Congress. In the conflict between employment and price stability, the cries of borrowers turned away, of big and little business mên, of veterans, of potential homeowners, of farmers, and above all of the unemployed, are forces against which the Federal Reserve cannot be insulated for long.[12]

[11] I have argued this case more fully in *Federal Reserve Policy-Making* (A. A. Knopf, New York, 1950), Chapters XI, XII, and XIII.

[12] Comparison with the British system of economic policy determination and execution provides interesting parallels and contrasts. Samuel H. Beer, who feels the British system of centralized informal intragovernmental economic leadership by the Treasury has worked very effectively, has analyzed this experience in *Treasury Control: The Coordination of Financial and Economic Policy in Great Britain* (Clarendon Press, Oxford, 1956). Beers comments on the whole process of compromising economic conflicts: "In American government the process of compromise is carried out largely in public—with much wear and tear on the nerves and some addition to the gaiety of existence. In Britain it is carried on behind the scenes. The pressures composed are on the whole less divisive and stubborn and the structure of government is less prone than the American to exacerbating and 'institutionalizing' conflict."

## V

On this note I should like to end. The problem of maintaining full employment without inflation has no easy answer. It would be intellectually satisfying to be able to close with a ringing pronouncement that all we need to do is protect the value of the dollar. But such pronouncements accomplish little. The job is to set clearly our long run goals, which I have argued should center around development of a firm tradition of price level stability, and at the same time to make the best use we can of such institutions as the Federal Reserve to fight inflation and to compromise effectively the pressures of diverse economic, ethical and political considerations in the America of today and tomorrow. Democracy is clearly not the most "efficient" form of government, and the democratic political process is open to use by self-seeking minority groups whose actions may turn the governmental process into an engine of inflation. Our hope is surely to fight vigorously for stable money at every turn, pushing forward as far as possible toward the better, widespread understanding of the illusory gains from inflationary income struggles that must be the real foundation for a successful stable money policy. In the meantime, we can hold to a reasonable minimum the real costs of unavoidable inflation through developing more inflation-protective social institutions for those passive economic groups who are most helplessly susceptible to the capricious erosion of rising prices.

# Index

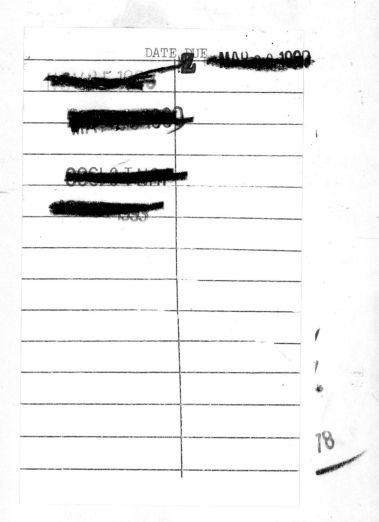